Houghton Mifflin Harcourt
Handwriting

Level A

Copyright © 2012 by Houghton Mifflin Harcourt Publishing Company

All rights reserved. No part of this work may be reproduced or transmitted in any form or by any means, electronic or mechanical, including photocopying or recording, or by any information storage or retrieval system, without the prior written permission of the copyright owner unless such copying is expressly permitted by federal copyright law.

Permission is hereby granted to individuals using the corresponding student's textbook or kit as the major vehicle for regular classroom instruction to photocopy Rubric and Handwriting Models from this publication in classroom quantities for instructional use and not for resale. Requests for information on other matters regarding duplication of this work should be addressed to Houghton Mifflin Harcourt Publishing Company, Attn: Contracts, Copyrights, and Licensing, 9400 South Park Center Loop, Orlando, Florida 32819.

Printed in the United States of America

ISBN 978-0-547-88243-7

20 0877 23

4500869425   A B C D E F G

If you have received these materials as examination copies free of charge, Houghton Mifflin Harcourt Publishing Company retains title to the materials and they may not be resold. Resale of examination copies is strictly prohibited.

Possession of this publication in print format does not entitle users to convert this publication, or any portion of it, into electronic format.

Contents

LESSON 1	The Lowercase Letters	2
LESSON 2	The Capital Letters	3
LESSON 3	Top, Middle, and Bottom	4
LESSON 4	Top to Bottom	5
LESSON 5	Left and Right	6
LESSON 6	Left to Right	7
LESSON 7	Alike and Different	8
LESSON 8	Which Ones are Alike?	9
LESSON 9	Letter Recognition	10
LESSON 10	Straight Letters	11
LESSON 11	Letter Shape	12
LESSON 12	Letter Size	14
LESSON 13	Letter and Word Spacing	16
LESSON 14	Smoothness	17
LESSON 15	Writing Numerals: Numerals 0, 1, 2	18
LESSON 16	Writing Numerals: Numerals 3, 4, 5	19
LESSON 17	Writing Numerals: Numerals 6, 7, 8	20
LESSON 18	Writing Numerals: Numerals 9, 10	21
LESSON 19	Numerals Practice	22
EVALUATION		23
LESSON 20	l	24
LESSON 21	L	25
LESSON 22	i	26
LESSON 23	I	27
LESSON 24	t	28
LESSON 25	T	29
LESSON 26	Practice	30
EVALUATION		31
LESSON 27	o	32
LESSON 28	O	33
LESSON 29	a	34
LESSON 30	A	35
LESSON 31	c	36
LESSON 32	C	37
LESSON 33	Practice	38
EVALUATION		39
LESSON 34	d	40
LESSON 35	D	41
LESSON 36	g	42
LESSON 37	G	43
LESSON 38	Practice	44
EVALUATION		45
LESSON 39	e	46
LESSON 40	E	47
LESSON 41	s	48
LESSON 42	S	49
LESSON 43	n	50
LESSON 44	N	51
LESSON 45	m	52

LESSON 46 M	53
LESSON 47 Practice	54
EVALUATION	55
LESSON 48 h	56
LESSON 49 H	57
LESSON 50 k	58
LESSON 51 K	59
LESSON 52 Using Punctuation: The Period	60
LESSON 53 Using Punctuation: The Question Mark	61
LESSON 54 b	62
LESSON 55 B	63
LESSON 56 p	64
LESSON 57 P	65
LESSON 58 Practice	66
EVALUATION	67
LESSON 59 r	68
LESSON 60 R	69
LESSON 61 f	70
LESSON 62 F	71
LESSON 63 u	72
LESSON 64 U	73
LESSON 65 w	74
LESSON 66 W	75
LESSON 67 Practice	76
EVALUATION	77
LESSON 68 y	78
LESSON 69 Y	79
LESSON 70 v	80
LESSON 71 V	81
LESSON 72 x	82
LESSON 73 X	83
LESSON 74 z	84
LESSON 75 Z	85
LESSON 76 Practice	86
EVALUATION	87
LESSON 77 q	88
LESSON 78 Q	89
LESSON 79 j	90
LESSON 80 J	91
LESSON 81 Handwriting Feature: Handwriting Problems	92
LESSON 82 Handwriting Feature: Personal Style	93
EVALUATION	94

Lesson 1

Name _____

The Lowercase Letters

a b c d

e f g h

i j k l

m n o p

q r s t

u v w x

y z

Lesson 2 Name _____

The Capital Letters

A B C D
E F G H
I J K L
M N O P
Q R S T
U V W X
Y Z

Lesson 3

Name _____

Top, Middle, and Bottom

Teacher's Directions: Tell students to circle the top bear, the middle cat, and the bottom fish.

4

Lesson 4 Name _____

Top to Bottom

Draw a line.

Teacher's Directions: Have students help each character get down by drawing a line from the dot near the word *top* to the dot near the word *bottom*.

5

Lesson 5 Name _____

Left and Right

Circle.

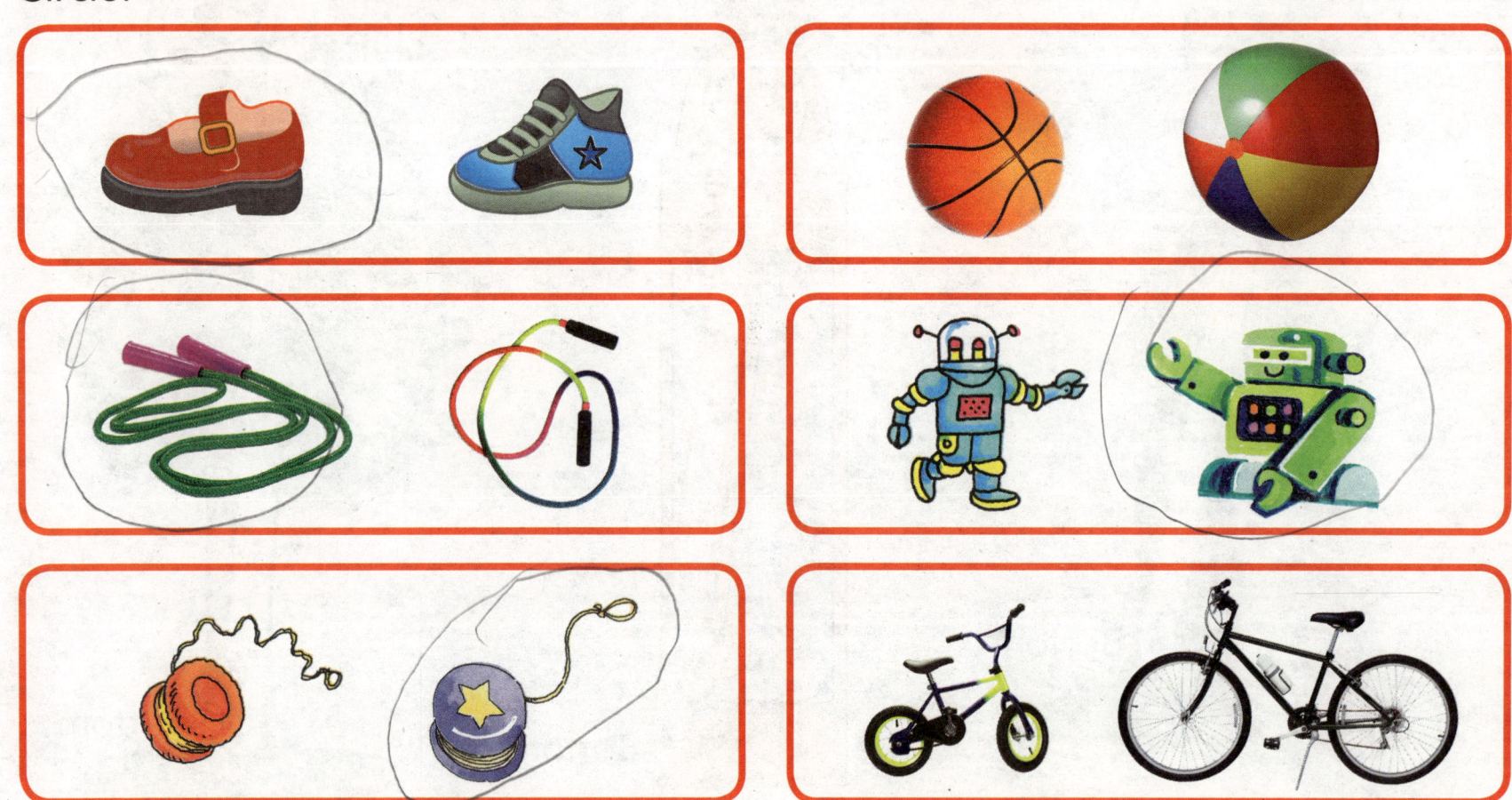

Teacher's Directions: For each pair of objects, direct students to circle the object on the left or to circle the object on the right.

Lesson 6

Name _____

Left to Right

Draw a line.

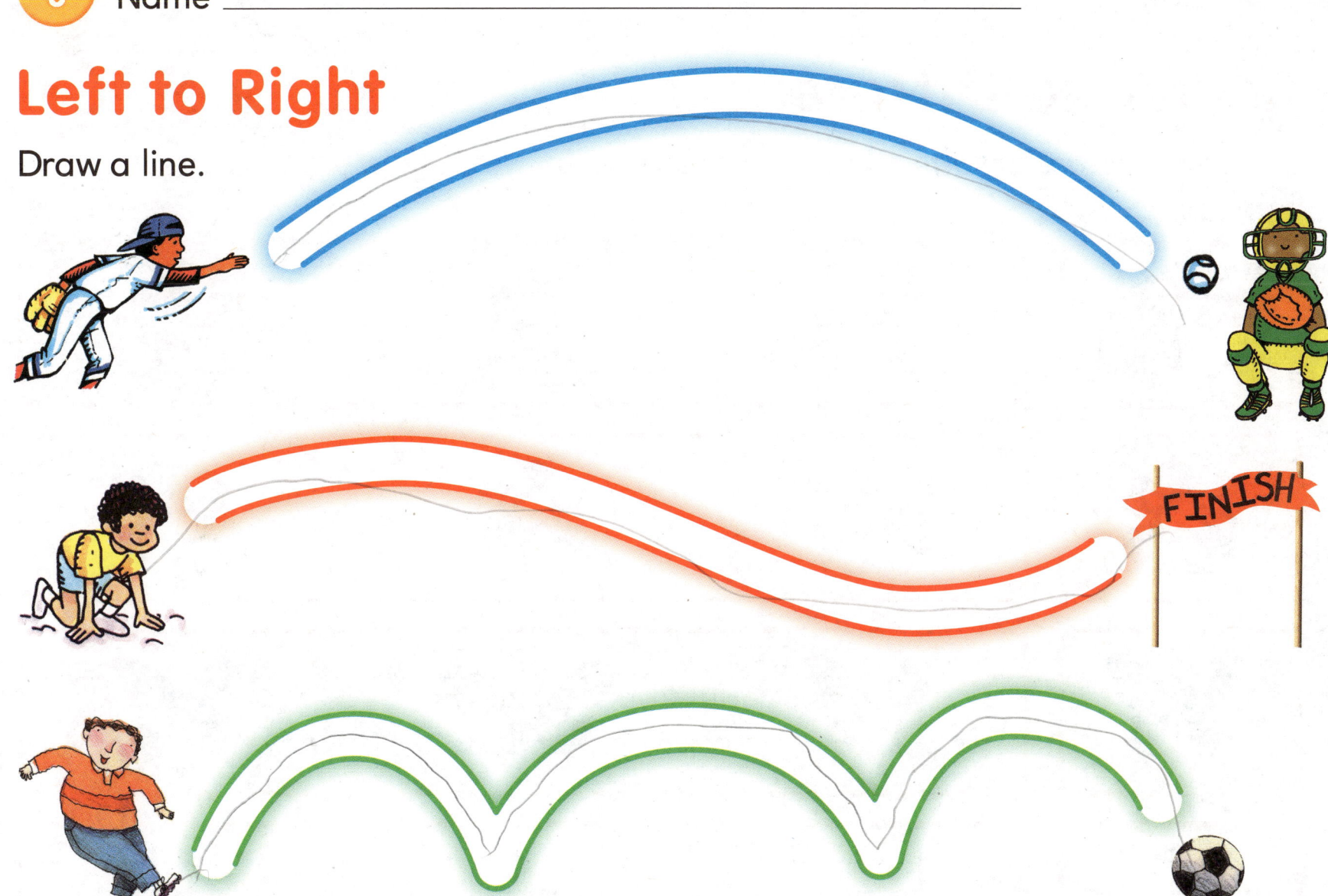

Teacher's Directions: Tell students to draw a line from left to right along each path.

Lesson 7 Name _____

Alike and Different

Circle the picture or letter that matches the one in the box.

d   b   p   d

8

Lesson 8

Name _____

Which Ones Are Alike?

Circle the letter that matches the one in the box.

c	e c o	S	X S Z
T	L F T	h	k h n
m	m n w	G	Q C G
B	E R B	g	g q y

Lesson 9

Letter Recognition

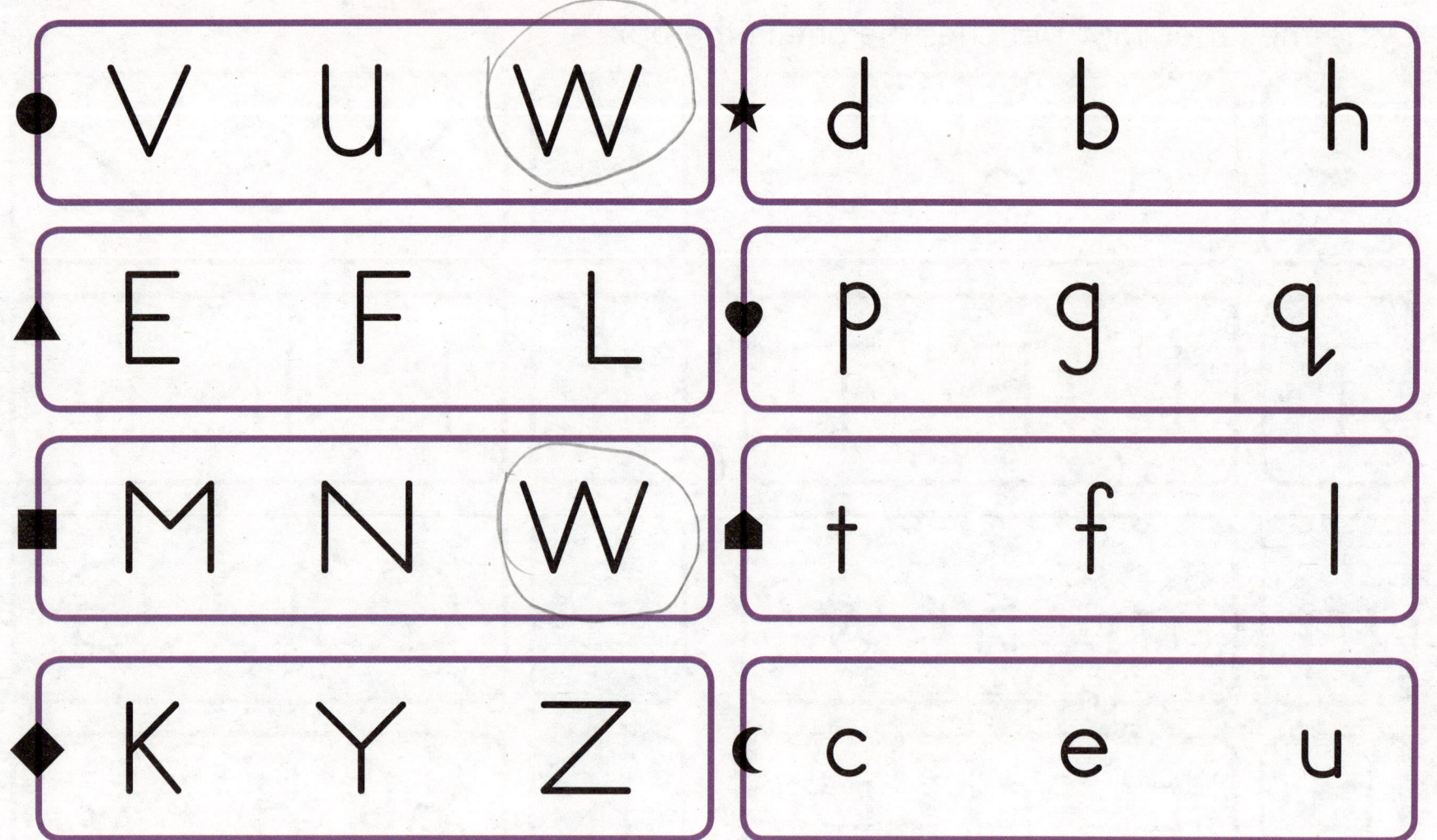

- V U (W)
- ★ d b h
- ▲ E F L
- ♥ p g q
- ■ M N (W)
- ♠ t f l
- ◆ K Y Z
- ☾ c e u

Teacher's Directions: Have students circle the following letters: **V, F, N, Z, b, q, t, e.**

10

Lesson 10 Name _____

Straight Letters

Some things are straight.

Some things slant.

In handwriting, letters should not slant.
All your letters should be straight from the top to the bottom.

My flowers grow tall.

Circle the letters that do not slant.

d i t m L B C F A

p s q r M R G N H

Lesson 11 | Name _____

Letter Shape

Here are the shapes you will need to write letters. In handwriting, these shapes are called **strokes**.

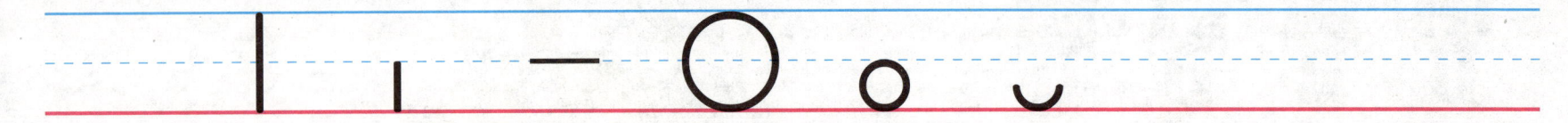

| I l — O o ᴗ

Look at the colored strokes in the letters below.

L T C R

Trace these letters.

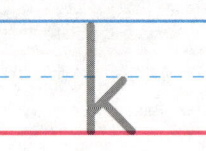

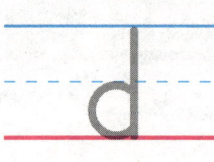

N m f Q k d

12

Lesson 11

Name _____

Trace and write each stroke.

Lesson 12

Name Willow

Letter Size

Top Line
Midline
Baseline
Descender Line

fog

Letters come in different sizes.

Some reach high.

These letters touch the top line and the baseline.

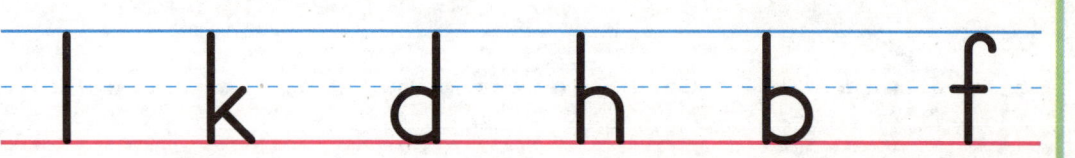

l k d h b f

Some sit low.

These letters touch the midline and the baseline.

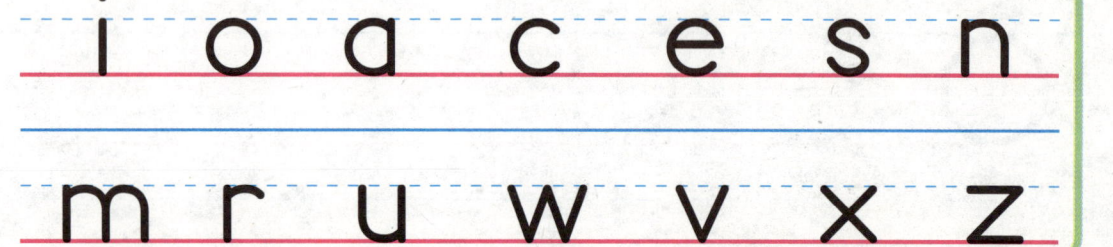

i o a c e s n

m r u w v x z

Some go below.

These letters touch the midline and the descender line.

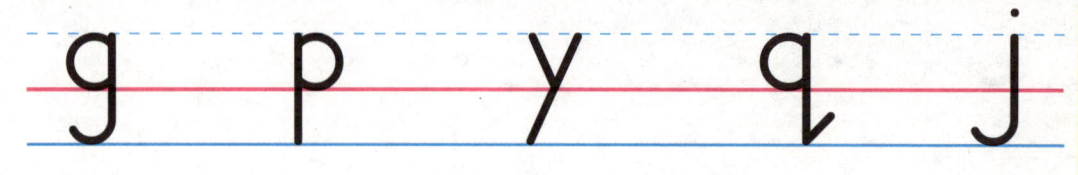

g p y q j

© Houghton Mifflin Harcourt Publishing Company

14

Lesson 12 Name _____

Reach High

l t k
d h b
f

Circle the letters that reach high.

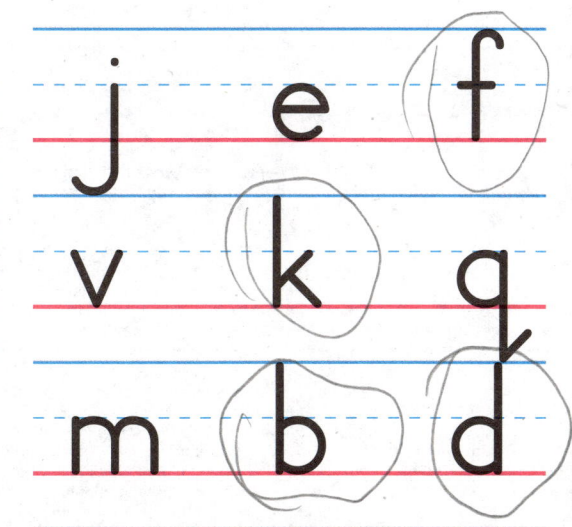

j e f
v k q
m b d

Sit Low

i o a c e
s n m r u
w v x z

Circle the letters that sit low.

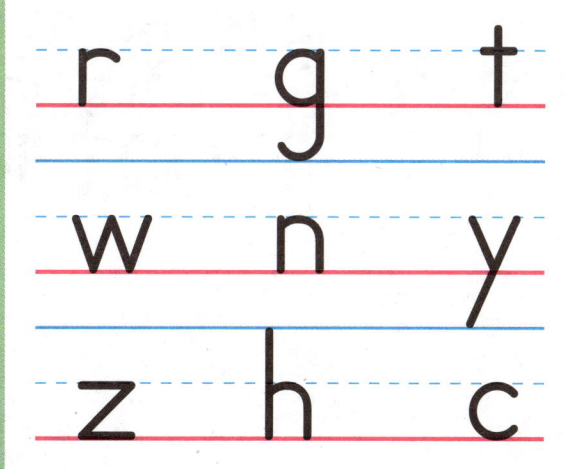

r g t
w n y
z h c

Go Below

g p y
q j

Circle the letters that go below.

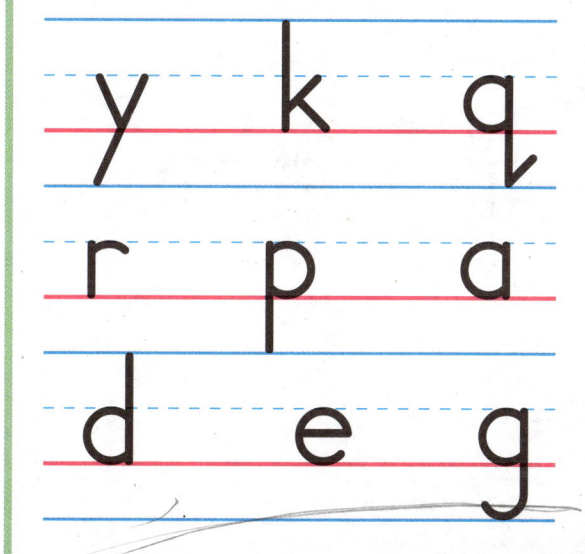

y k q
r p a
d e g

15

Lesson 13 Name _____

Letter and Word Spacing

Leave the space of a pencil point between letters.

Correct

just right

Incorrect

tooclose

too far

Leave the space of a pencil between words.

Correct

like this

Incorrect

not like   this

16

Smoothness

Good handwriting is smooth.
The lines are even and flowing.

Tell which handwriting is best.

too light

shaky

too dark

too thick

just right

Lesson 15 Writing Numerals

Name Willow

Numerals 0, 1, 2

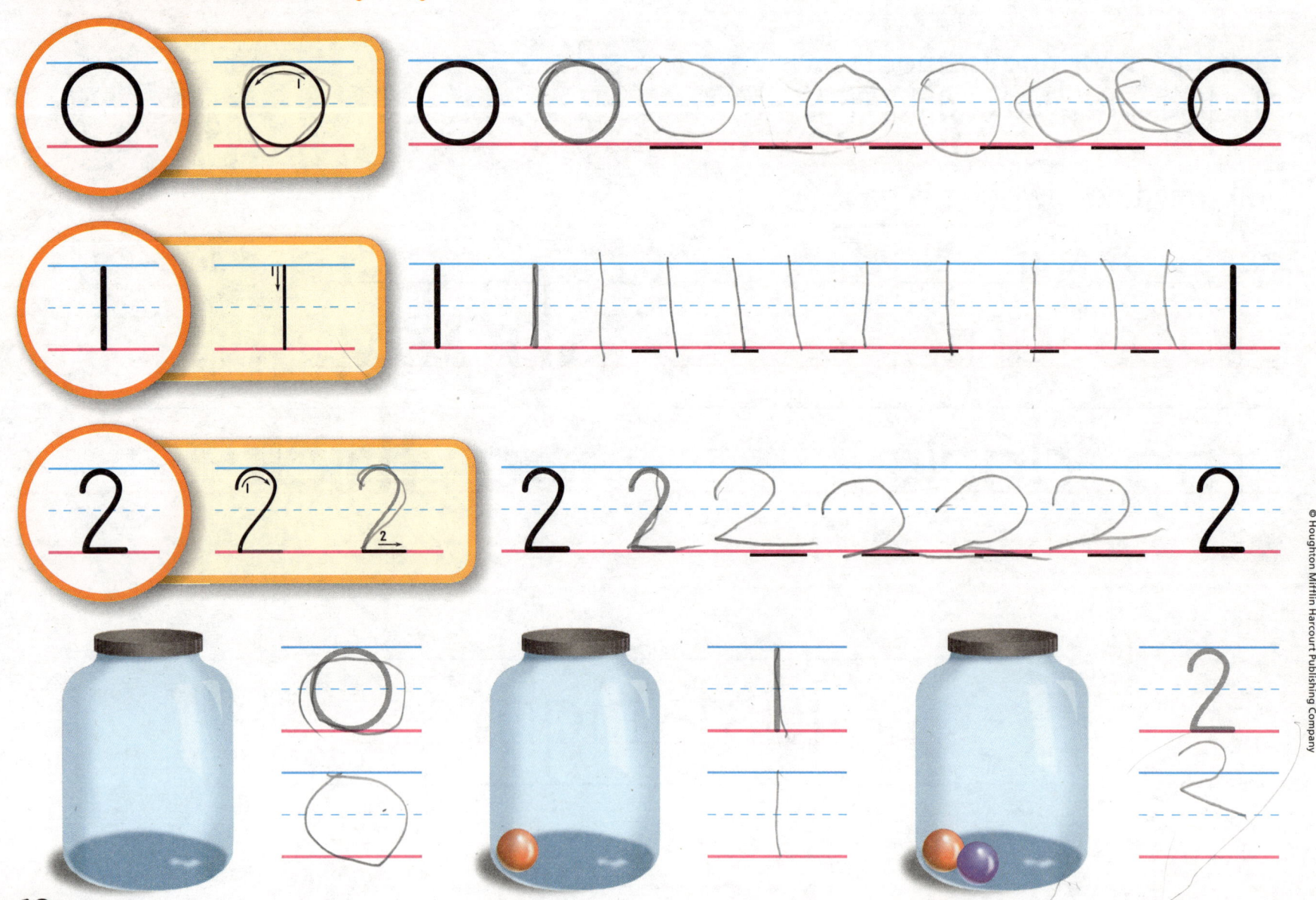

Lesson 16 Writing Numerals

Name _____

Numerals 3, 4, 5

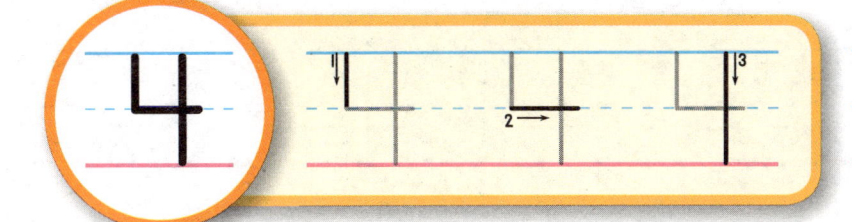

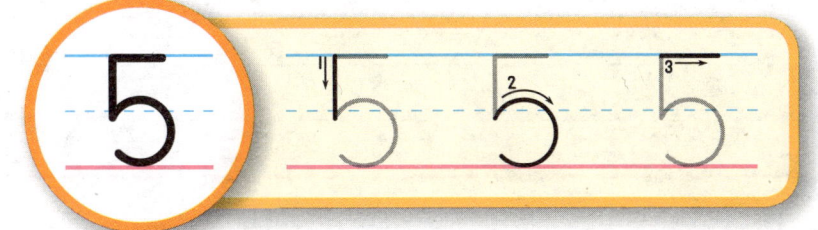

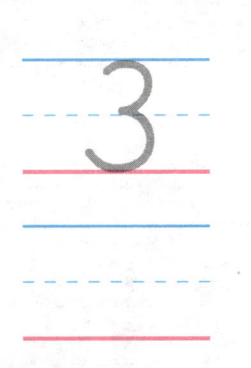

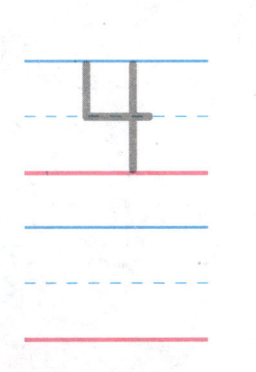

Lesson 17 **Writing Numerals**

Name _____

Numerals 6, 7, 8

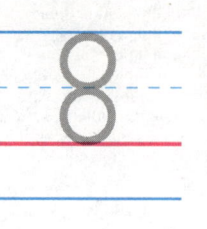

Lesson 18 — **Writing Numerals**

Name _____

Numerals 9, 10

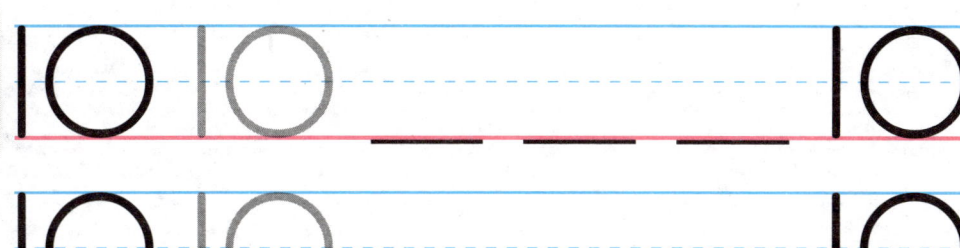

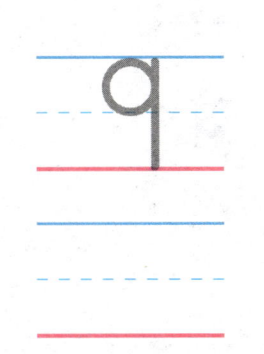

Lesson 19 Practice

Name _____

0

1

2

3

4

5

6

7

8

9

Teacher's Directions: Have students write each numeral.

Evaluation Name _____

Circle the words that are written correctly.

bat   ball   mitt   cap

Circle the letters that reach high.
Underline the letters that go below.

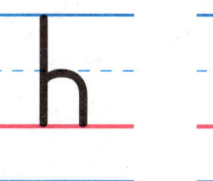

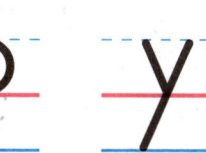

s   h   j   o   y   l

good w or k   good work

Lesson 20

Name _____

learn   help   talk   play

_earn   he_p   ta_k   p_ay

24   Self Check   Circle your best l.

Lesson 21

Name _____

L

Look at us learn.
_ook at us _earn.

Speaking and Listening Tell something you have learned at school this year.

25

Lesson 22　Name _____

i　　i　　i i i i i i

i i i

i i i

i i i

paint　fish　kite　scissors
pa_nt　f_sh　k_te　sc_ssors

26　**Self Check** Circle your best i.

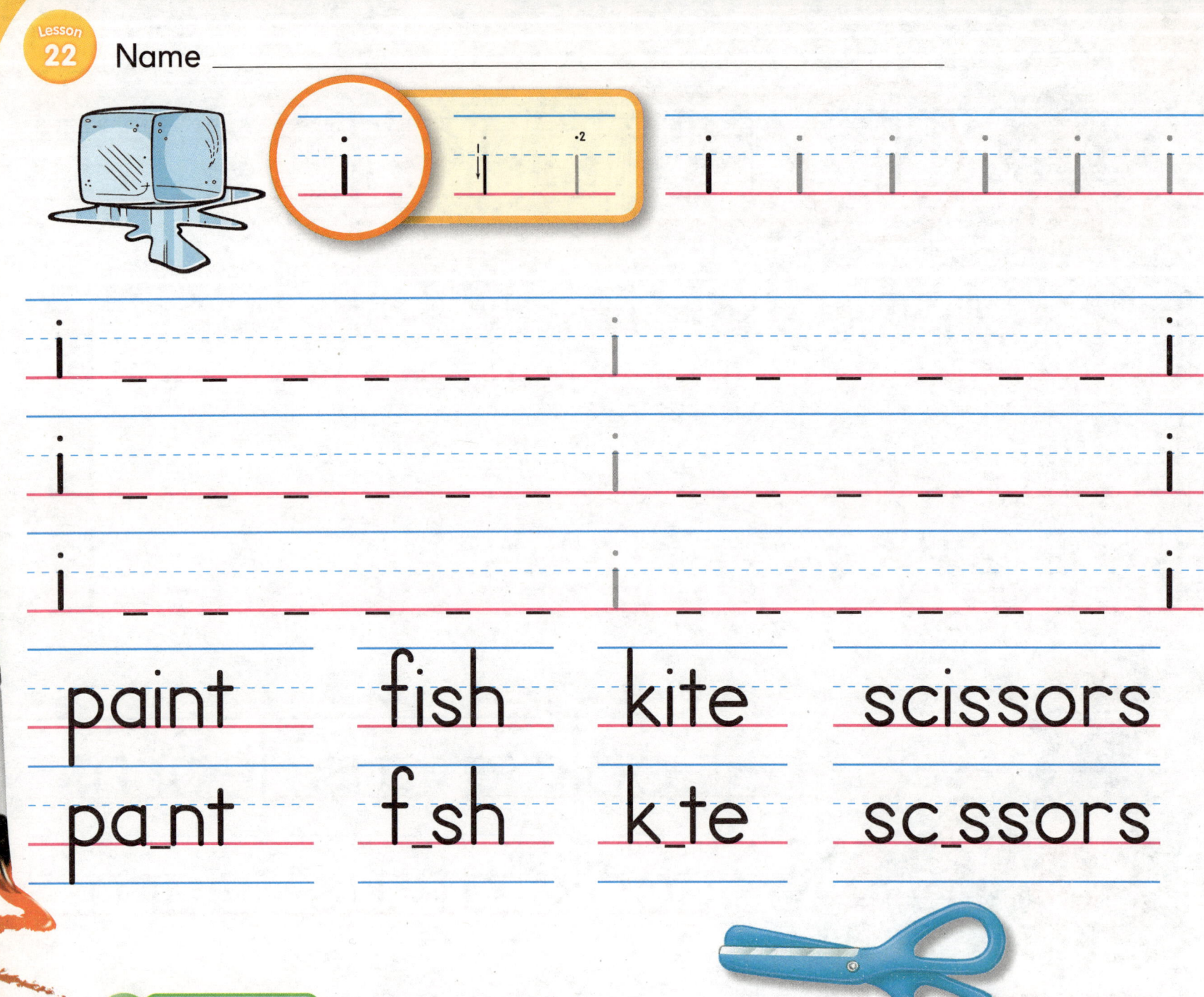

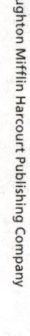

Lesson 23 Name _____

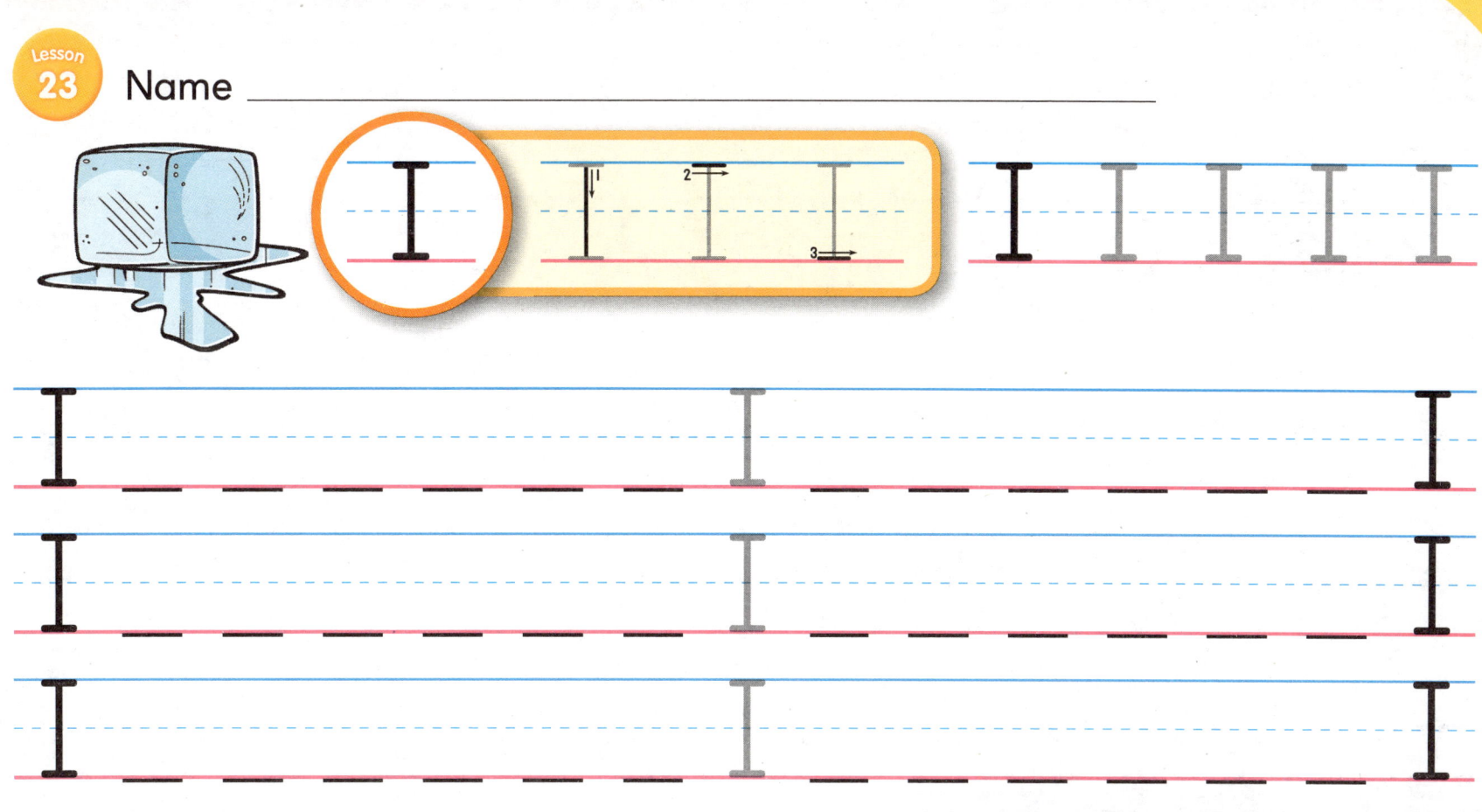

I I I I I I

I I I

I I I

I I I

I like rainbows.

I lke ranbows.

Speaking and Listening Tell what you like to draw or paint.

27

Lesson 24

Name _____

t t t t t t t t

t							t

t							t

t							t

teacher tells stories

_eacher _e_s s_or_es

28 **Self Check** Circle a t that touches the top line and the baseline.

Lesson 25 Name _____

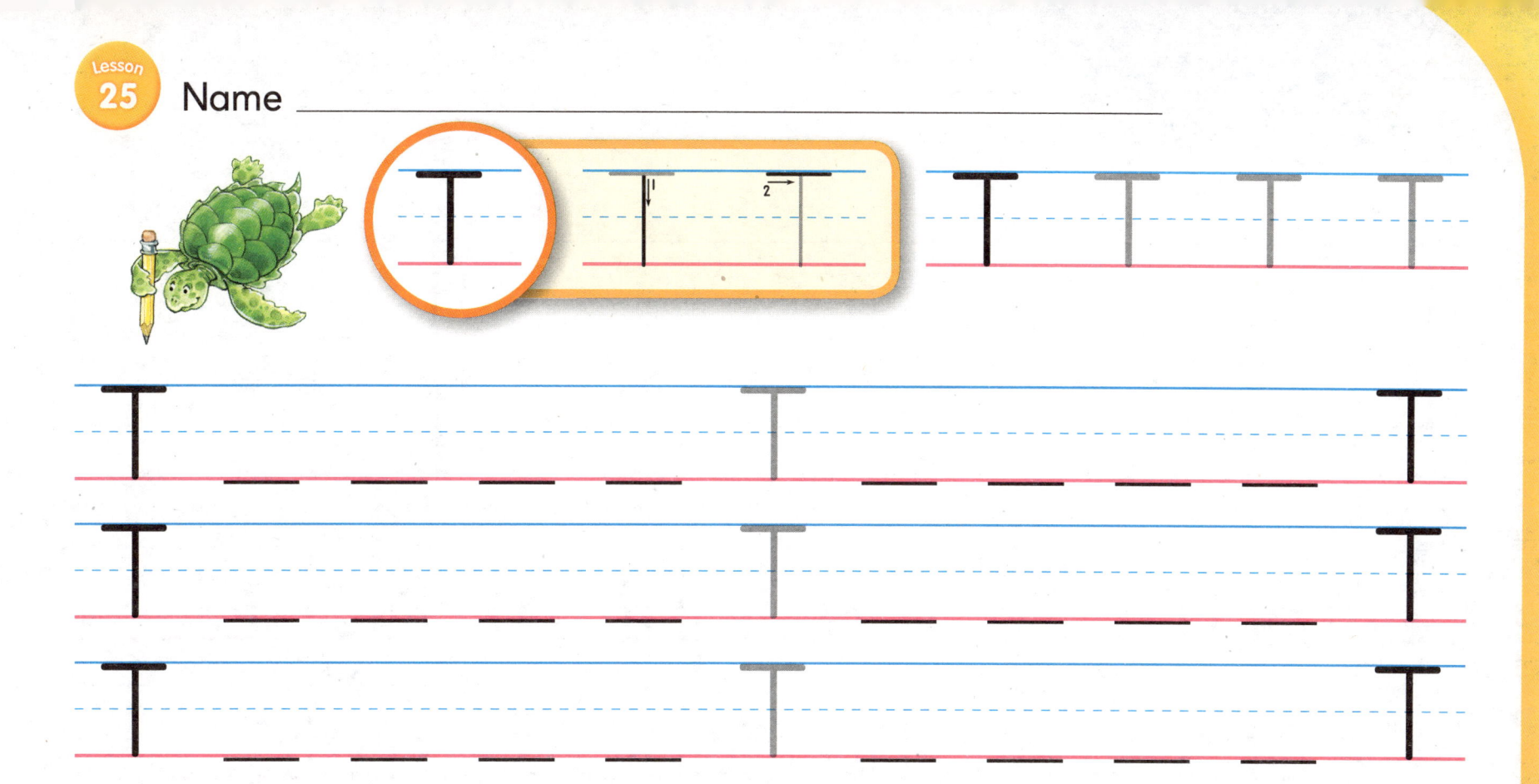

Timothy likes to read.
_imo_hy _kes _o read.

Speaking and Listening Tell what you like to do at school.

29

Lesson 26 Practice   Name _____

l
L

i
I

t
T

I turn off the light at night.
_urn off _he _gh_ a_ n gh_.

Teacher's Directions: Have students write the missing letters.

Evaluation   Name _____

Write the letters and words.

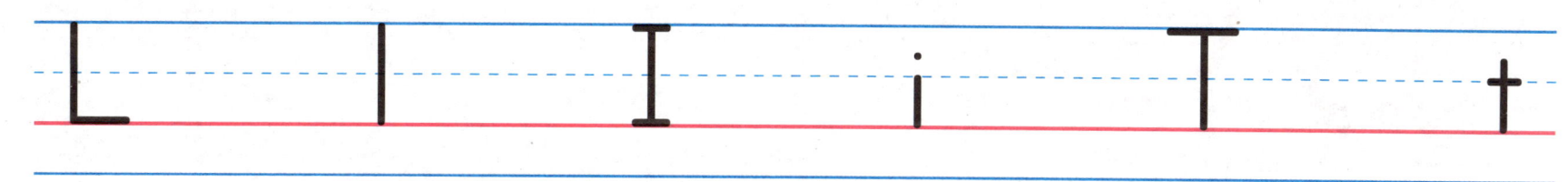

L   I   I   i   T   t

Circle the letter you wrote best.

Circle the word you wrote best.

it   lit   ill

31

Lesson 27

Name _____

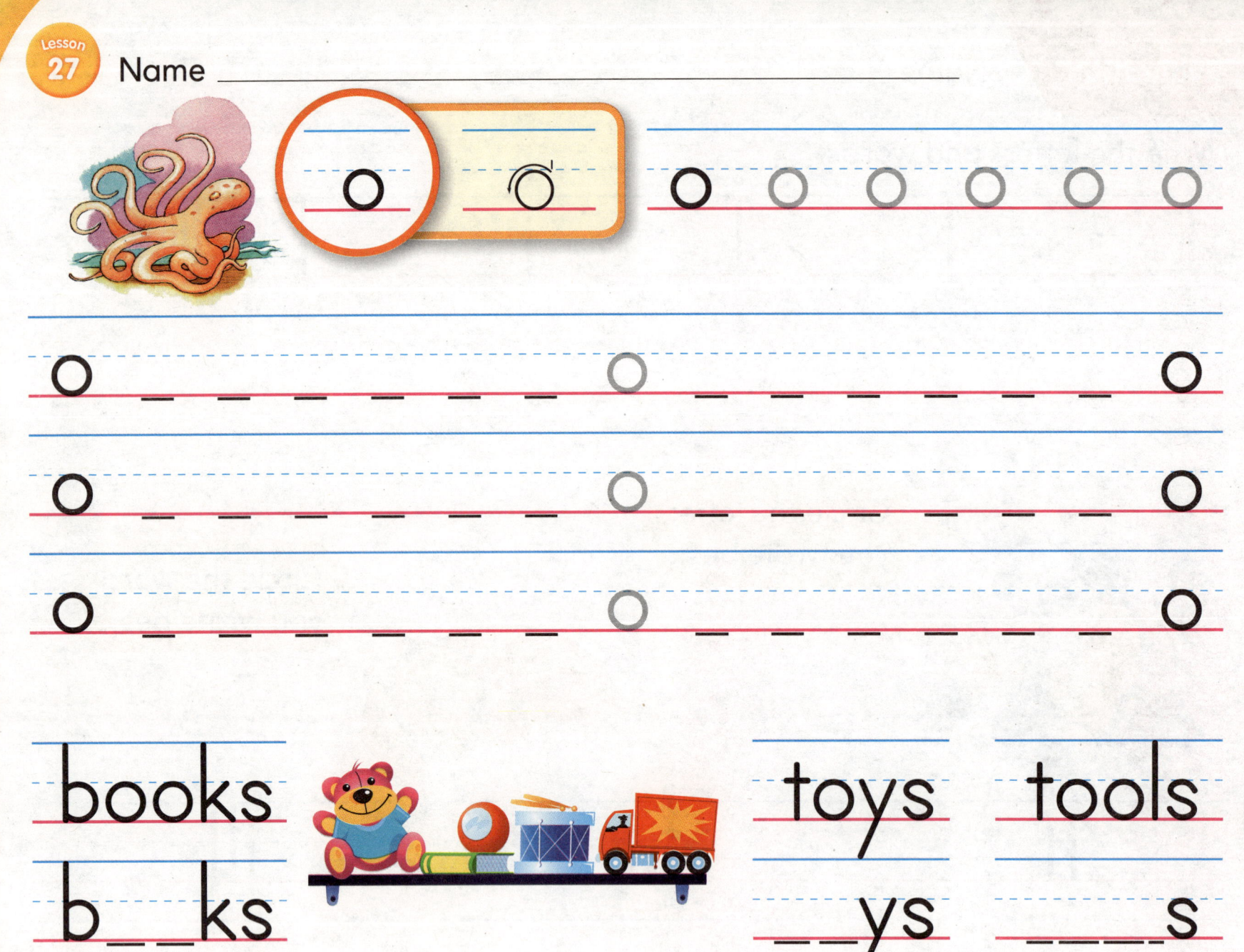

O o o o o o o o

books
b_ _ks

toys
_ _ys

tools
_ _ _s

32 Speaking and Listening — Tell about a list you have made.

Lesson 28

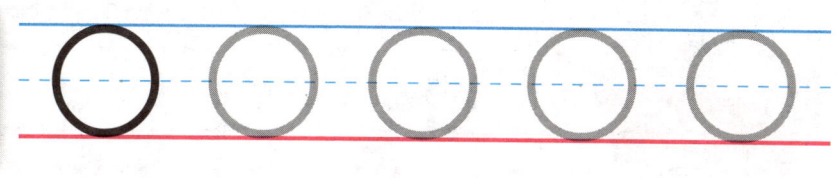

Name _____

O O O O O O O

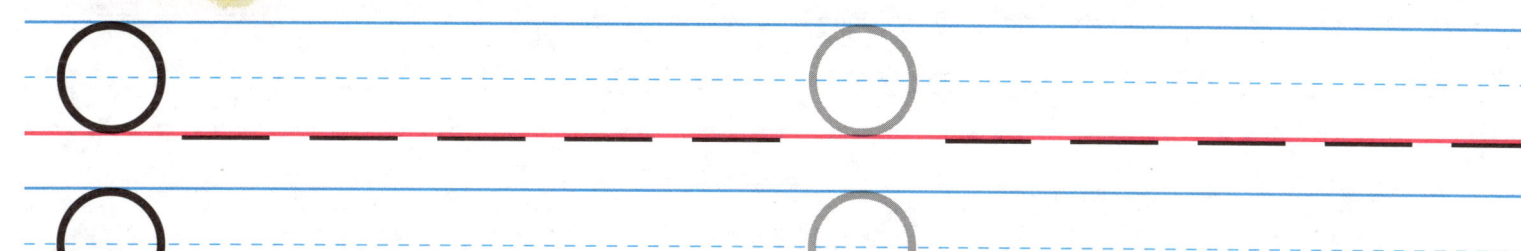

O   O   O

O   O   O

Olga   Olivia   Oscar

__ga   __via   __scar

▶ **Ask a Friend** Have a friend circle your best O.

33

Lesson 29

Name _____

a a a a a a a a a

a a a

a a a

a a a

alligator   seal   bear

___g___r   se__   be_r

34 **Self Check** Circle your best a.

Lesson 30 Name _____

A A A A A A A

A   A   A

A   A   A

A   A   A

Alligators are amazing.

___ ___ ___ g ___ ___ rs ___ re ___ m ___ z ___ ng.

Speaking and Listening Name an animal you think is amazing. Tell why.

35

Lesson 31 Name _____

C c

C c c c c c c

c　　　　　c　　　　c

c　　　　　c　　　　c

c　　　　　c　　　　c

carrots　　corn　　lettuce

_ _ rr _ s　_ _ rn　_ e _ u _ e

36 On Your Own Make a list of vegetables you like to eat.

Lesson 32 Name _____

C C C C C C C C

C C C

C C C

C C C

Carol plants a garden.

__ r __ p __ nt __ g __ rden.

Have a friend circle your best C and tell why it is best.

Ask a Friend

37

Lesson 33 Practice Name _____

o _ _ _ _   a _ _ _ _   c _ _ _ _
O _ _ _ _   A _ _ _ _   C _ _ _ _

I wear a coat outside.
I we_r _ _ _ _ t ou_side.

Teacher's Directions: Have students write the missing letters.

38

Evaluation   Name _____

Write the letters and words.

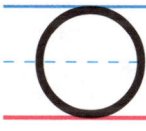

O   o   A   a   C   c

Circle the letter you wrote best.

cat   cool   tall

Circle the word you wrote best.

Lesson 34 Name _____

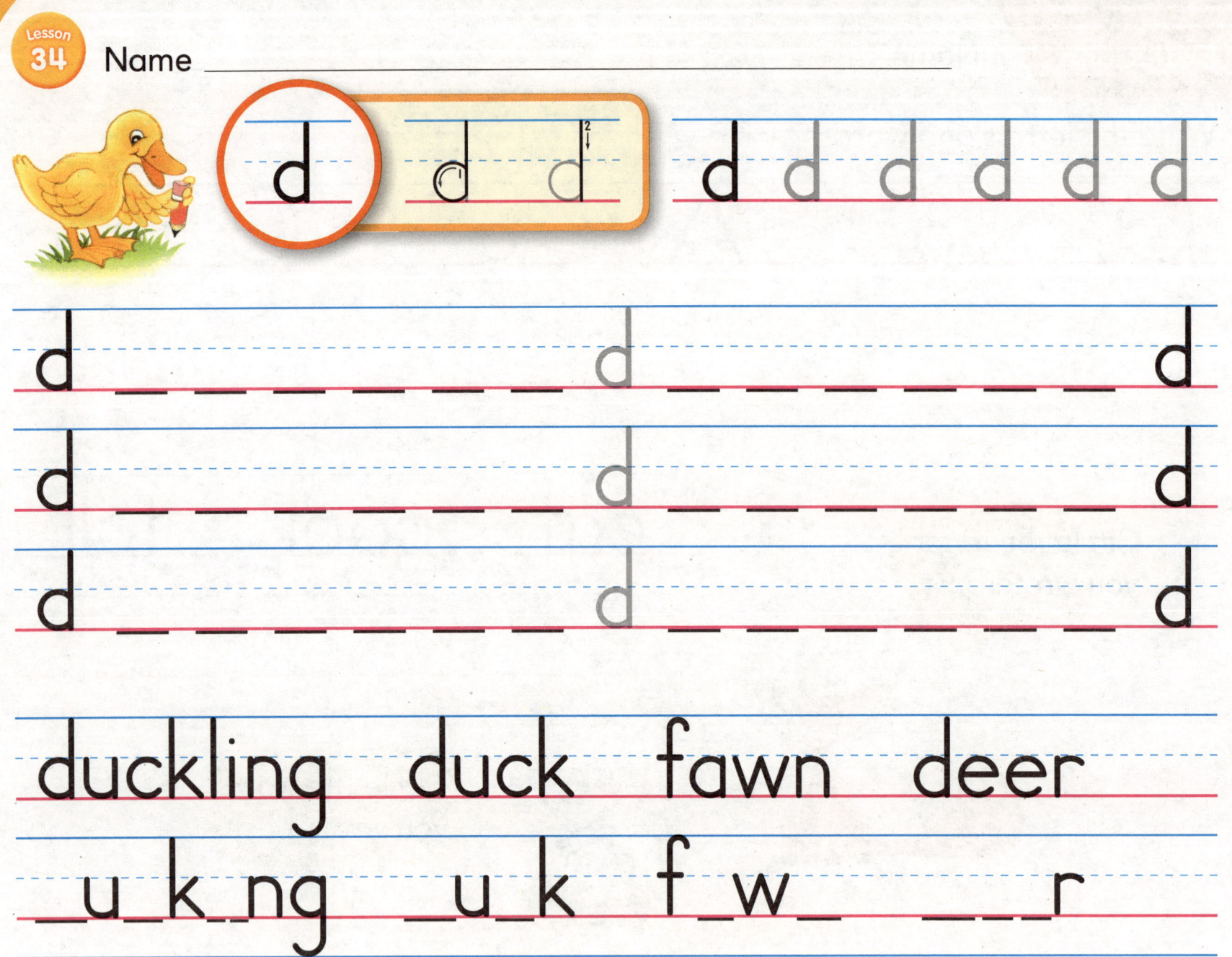

d d d d d d d d

d d d

d d d

d d d

duckling duck fawn deer
_u_k_ng _u_k f_w_ __r

40 **Self Check** Circle your best d.

Lesson 35

Name _____

D D D D D D D D D

D D D

D D D

D D D

Do ducklings dive?

_ u k_ngs _ve?

▶ Speaking and Listening Tell what you would like to learn about ducklings.

41

Lesson 36   Name _____

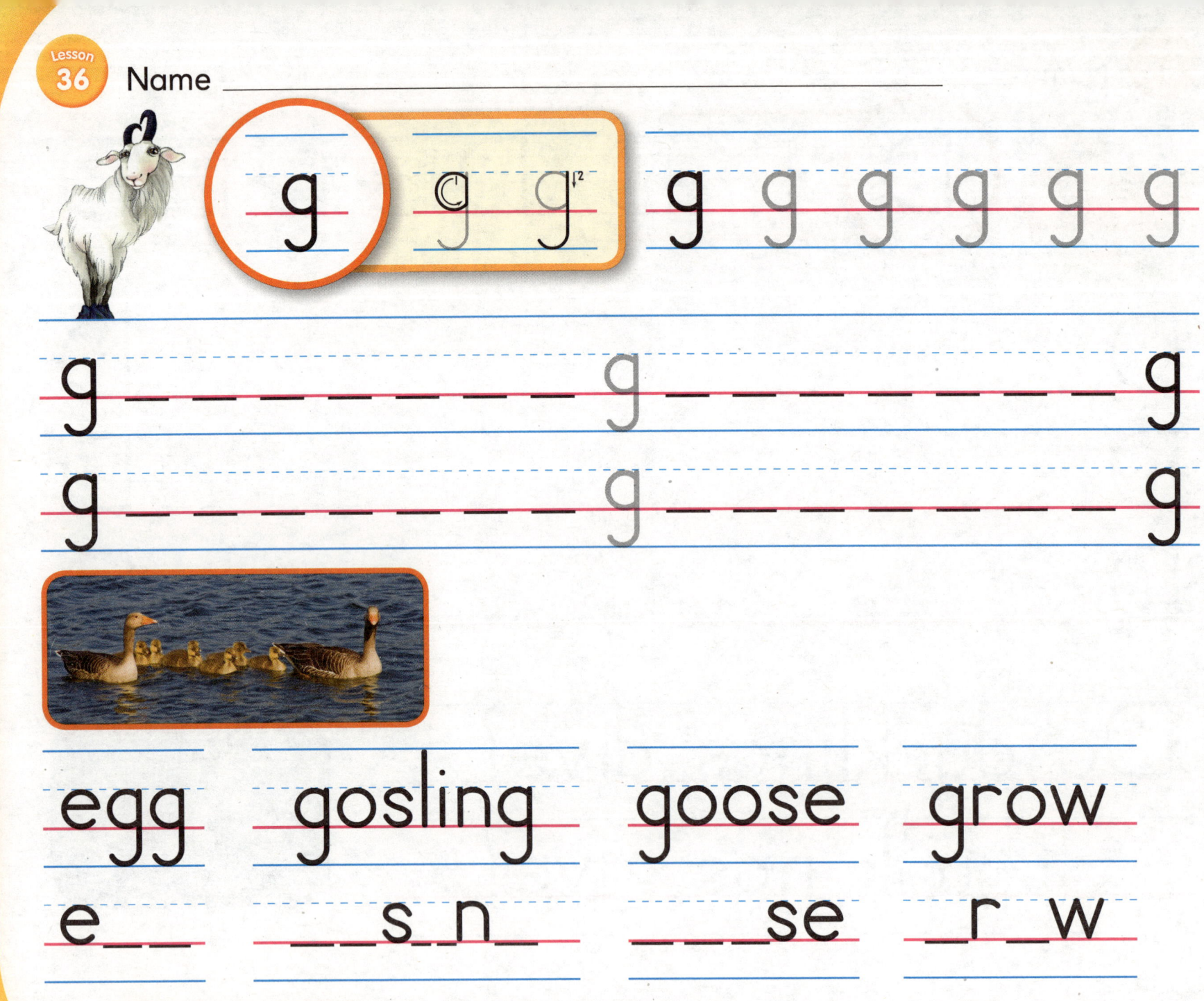

g g g g g g g g g g

g   g   g
g   g   g

egg   gosling   goose   grow
e__   __s__n   ___se   _r_w

42 Ask a Friend Have a friend circle your best g.

Lesson 37

Name _____

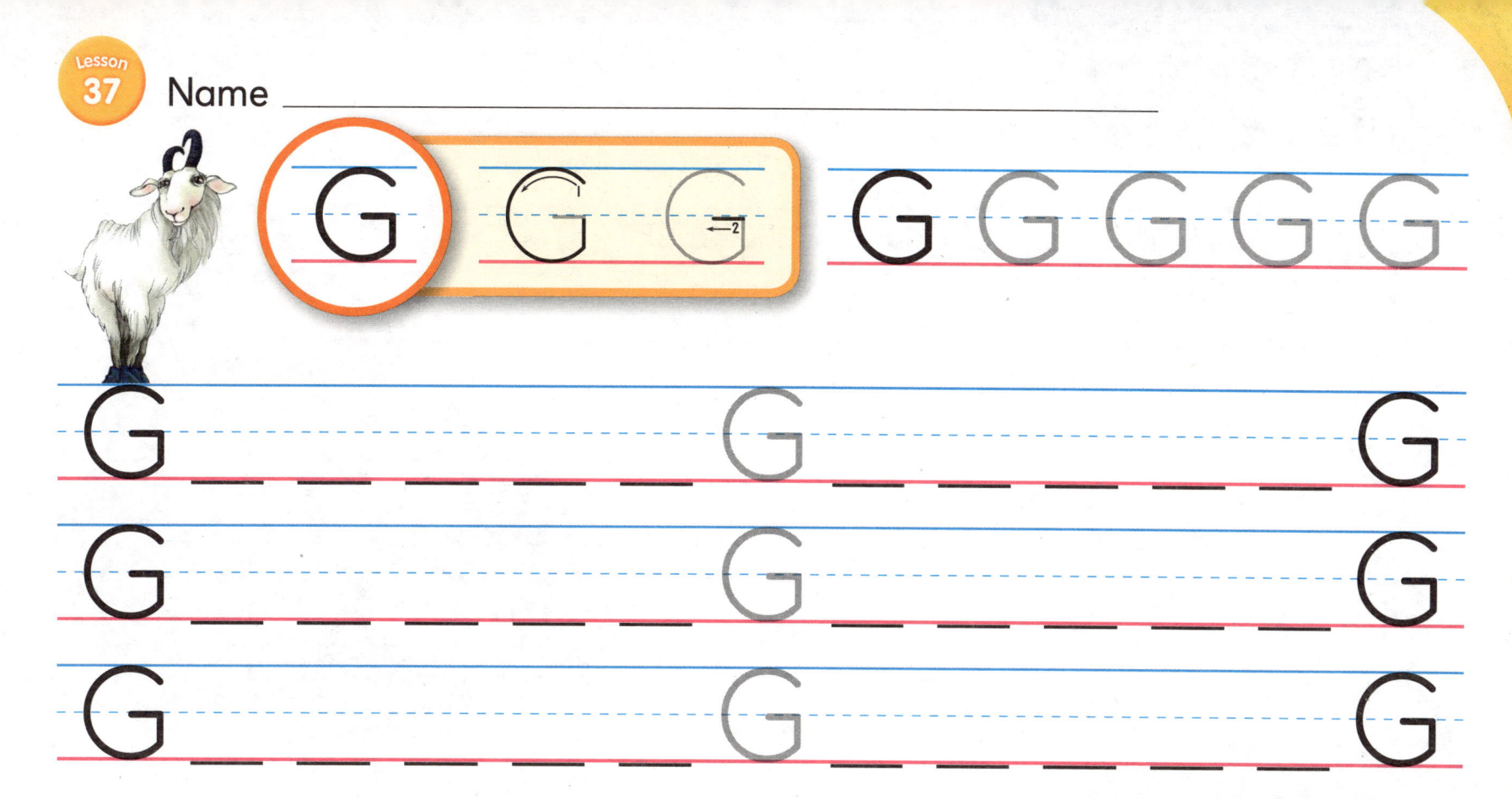

G G G G G G G G G

G G G

G G G

G G G

Goslings eat grain.
___s_ngs e___ r_n.

Speaking and Listening Share another fact about baby birds.

43

Lesson 38 Practice Name _____

d _____

D _____

g _____

G _____

My dog likes to go for a ride.
My _o_ lkes _o _o f r a r _ e.

Teacher's Directions: Have students write the missing letters.

44

Evaluation Name _____

Trace each word. Then write the word.

dog   goat   toad

Gil   Dot   Gail

bat   Todd   lot

Circle a word in which all the letters slant the same way.

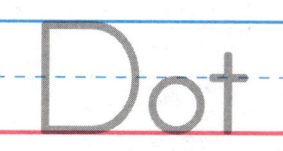

Circle the word you wrote best.

45

Lesson 39

Name _____

e e e e e e e e

e e e

e e e

e e e

elephant

__ph_n__

giraffe

_r_ff

46 **Self Check** Circle your best e.

Lesson 40 Name _____

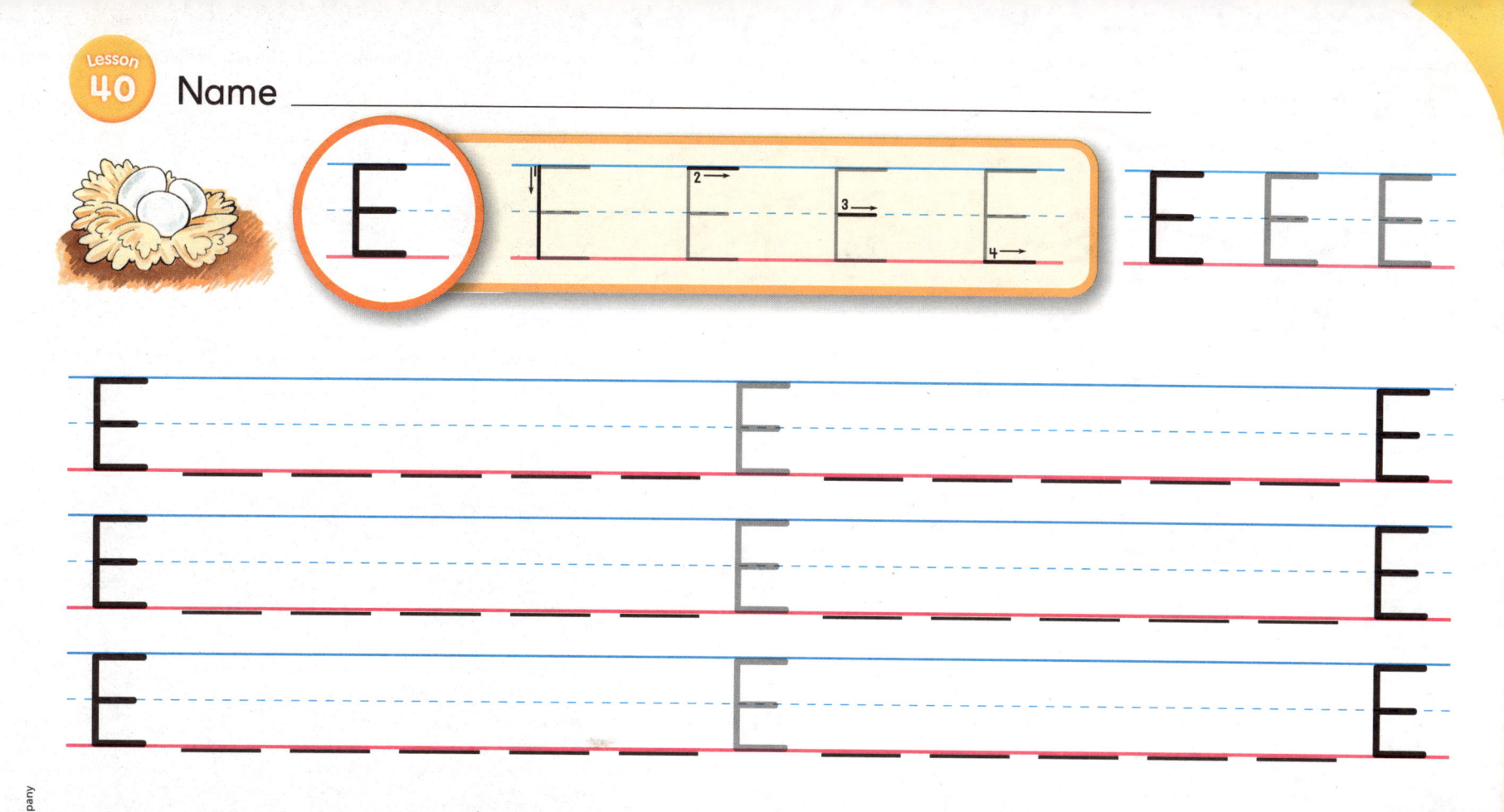

E   E E E E   E E E

E   E   E

E   E   E

E   E   E

Every elephant can swim.

_v_ry ___ph_n_ __n sw_m.

Speaking and Listening Share what you know about elephants.

47

Lesson 41

Name _____

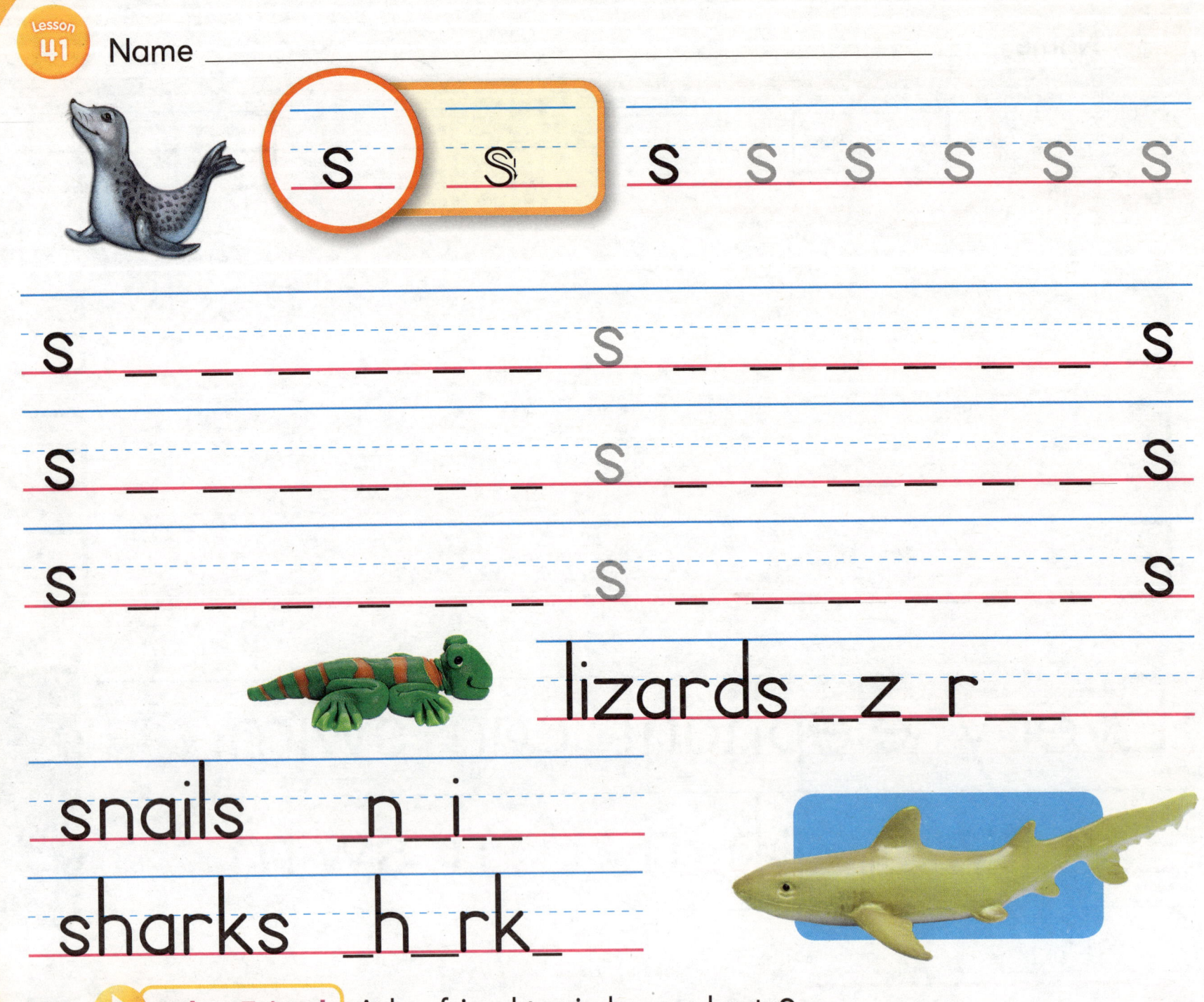

S s   S s   S s S s S s S s

S   S   S

S   S   S

S   S   S

lizards _z_r_

snails _n_i_

sharks _h_rk_

Ask a Friend — Ask a friend to circle your best S.

Lesson 42 Name _____

S S S S S S S S

S S S

S S S

S S S

Snakes shed their skins.

_n_k_ _h_ _h_r_ _kn_.

Speaking and Listening Tell something you know about snakes or other reptiles.

49

Lesson 43

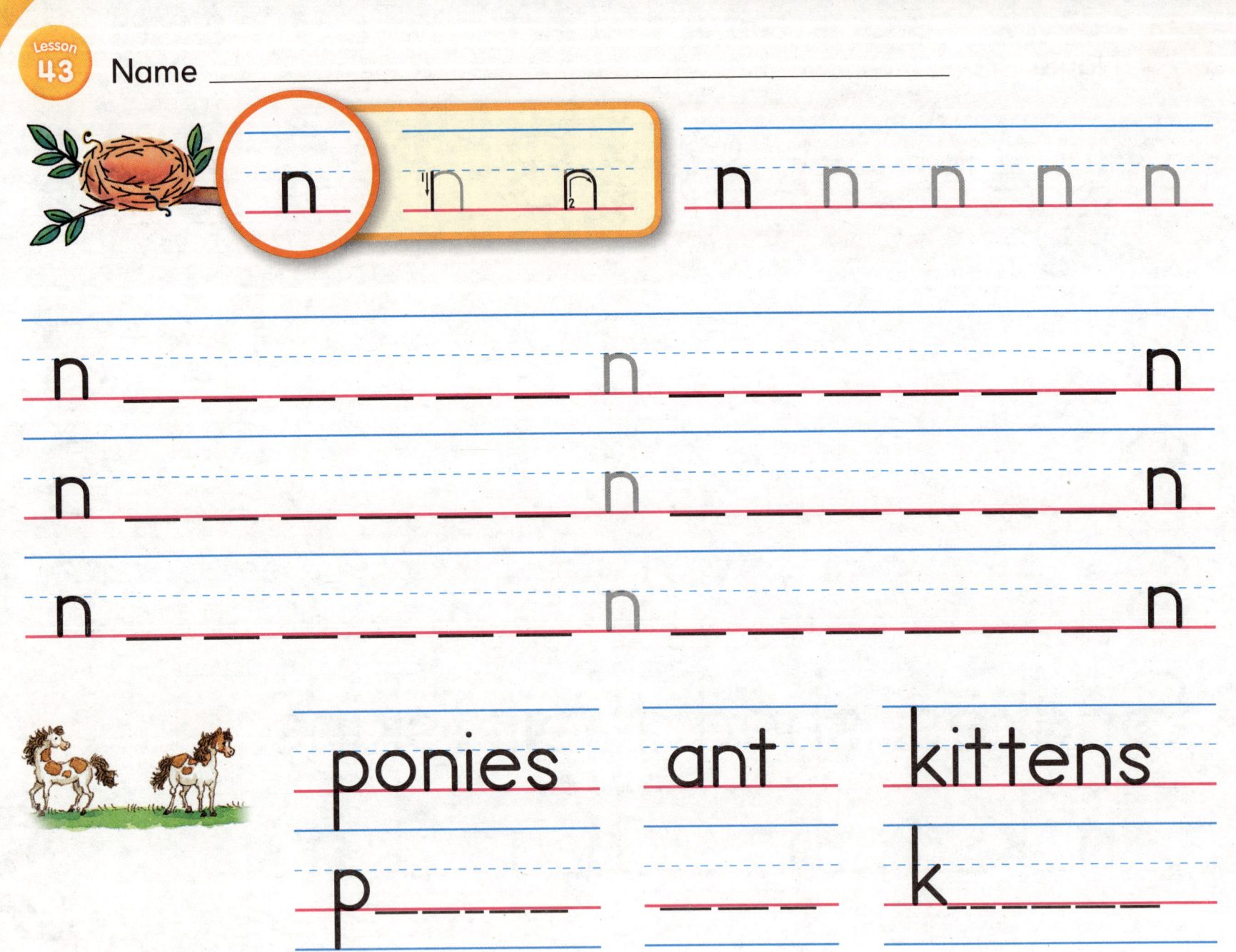

Name _____

n n n n n n n

n n n

n n n

n n n

ponies   ant   kittens

p____   ____   k____

50 **Speaking and Listening** Tell a friend about your favorite animal.

Lesson 44

Name _____

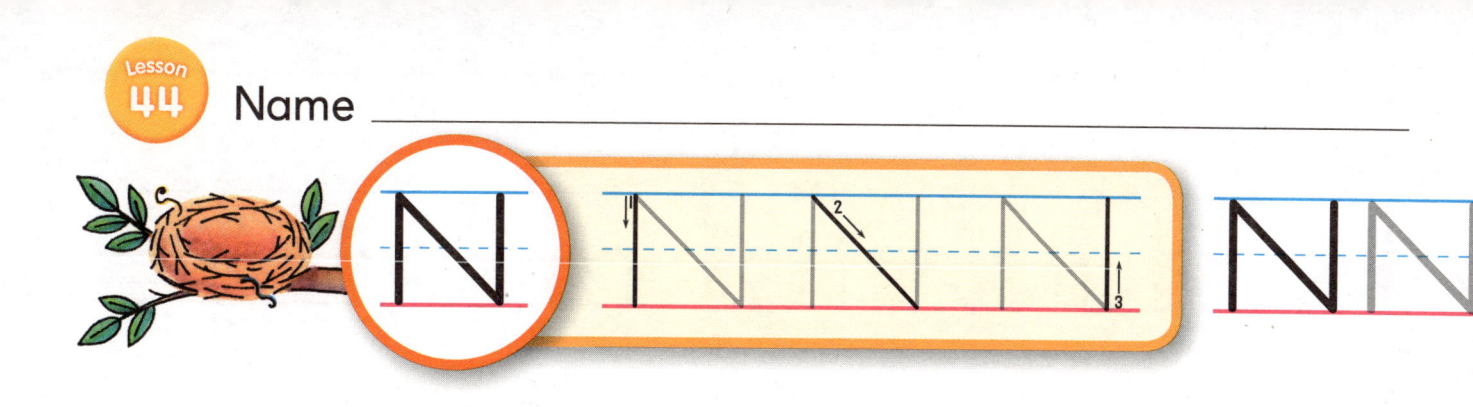

N N N N N   N N N N

N   N   N
N   N   N

Neil wants a kitten.
    w_____ k_____.
No one else does.
_____.

Self Check Circle the N you wrote best.

51

Lesson 45

Name _____

m   m m m   m   m   m

m   m   m

m   m   m

m   m   m

monkey   el mono

___ ___ k y   ___ ___ ___ ___

Ask a friend to circle your best m and underline an m that needs work.

52 Ask a Friend

Lesson 46

Name _____

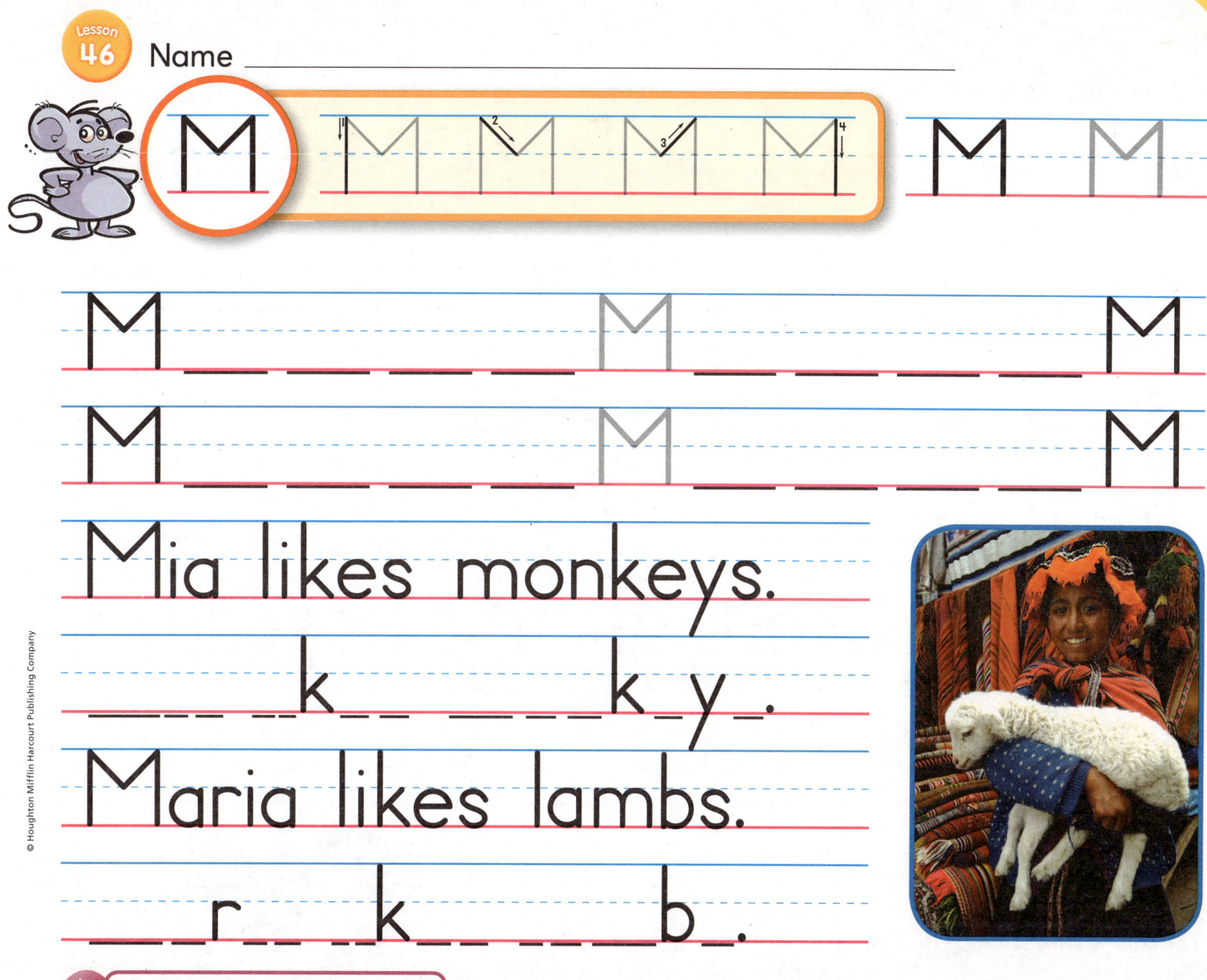

M M M M M M M M

M M M
M M M

Mia likes monkeys.
__ __ k __ __ __ k y.

Maria likes lambs.
__ r __ k __ __ b __.

Speaking and Listening Tell what animal you like best.

53

Lesson 47 Practice

Name _____

e _____   E _____

n _____   N _____

s _____   S _____

m _____   M _____

Snow fell on my nose.

_____ w f _____ y ___ .

Teacher's Directions: Have students write the missing letters.

54

Evaluation Name _____

Trace each word. Then write the word.

ants   snails   eels

camels   Nina   Matt

Santo   Naomi

Circle the word you wrote best.

Circle a word in which all the letters slant the same way.

55

Lesson 48

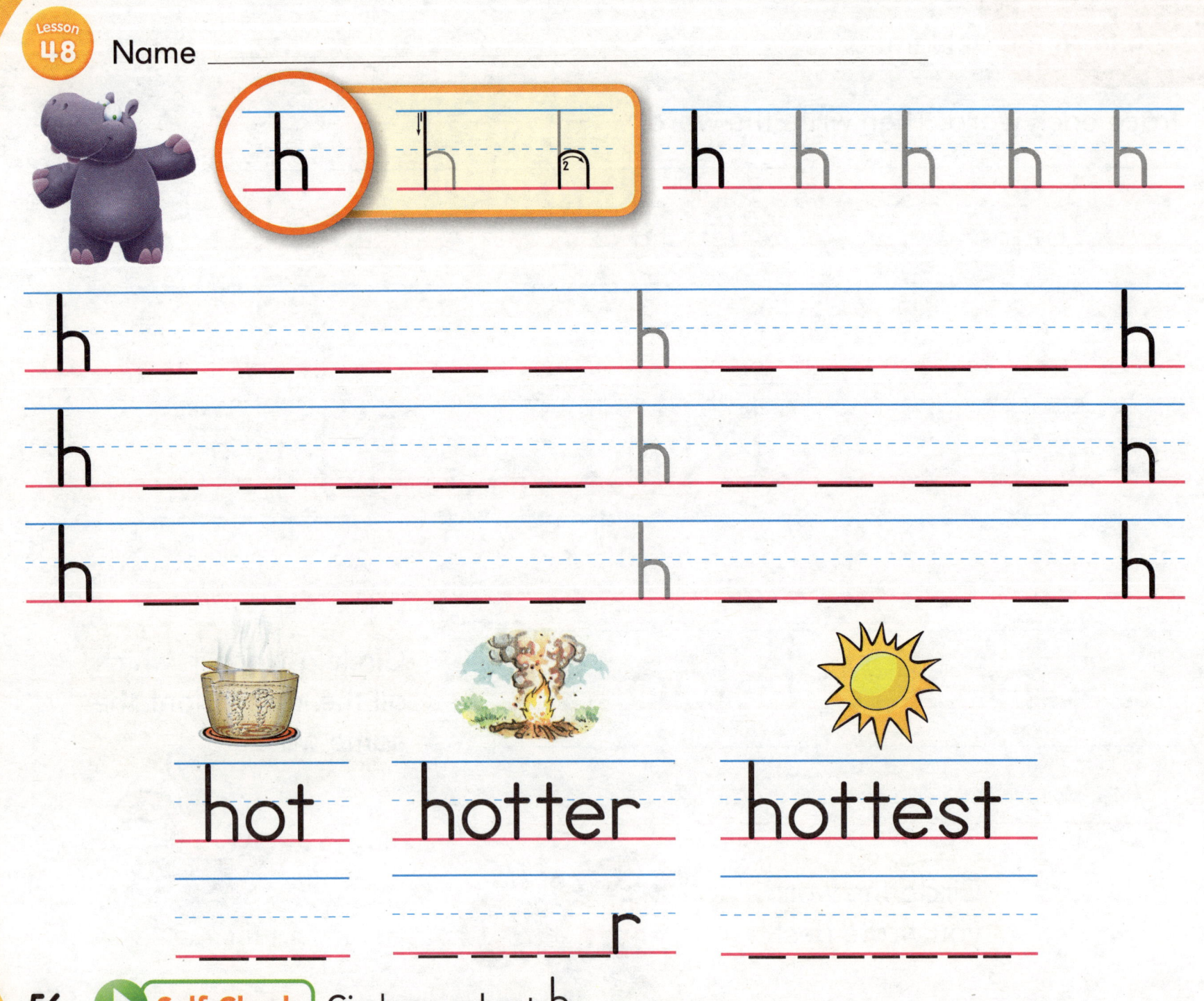

Name _____

h h h h h h h h

h　　　　　　　　h　　　　　　h

h　　　　　　　　h　　　　　　h

h　　　　　　　　h　　　　　　h

hot　　　hotter　　　hottest

___　　　___r　　　___

56　Self Check　Circle your best h.

Lesson 49

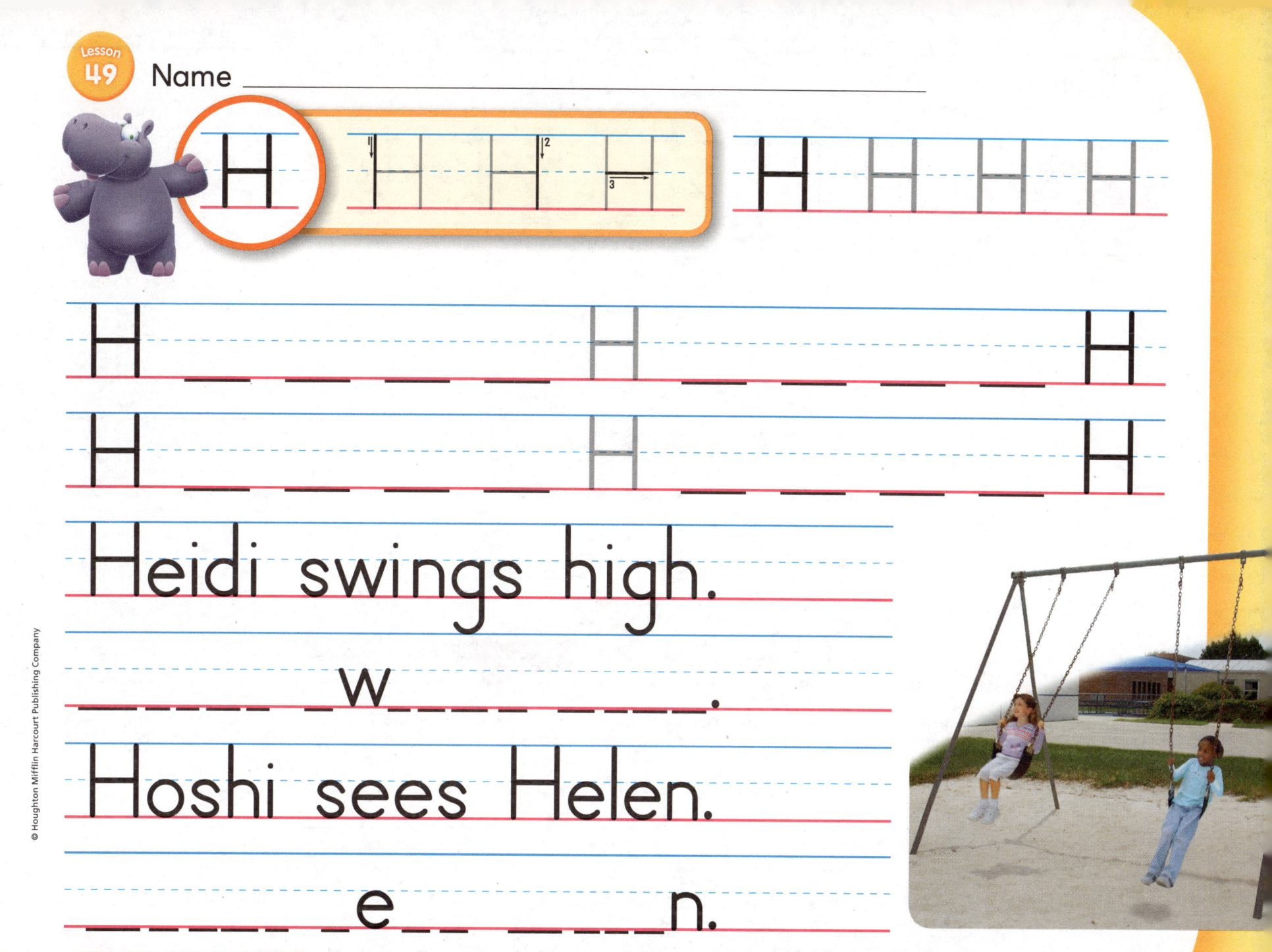

Name _____

H H H H   H H H H

H   H   H
H   H   H

Heidi swings high.
___ ___ w_____.
Hoshi sees Helen.
_____ e_____ n.

▶ **On Your Own** Draw pictures to explain the words *light, lighter, lightest*.

57

Lesson 50

Name _____

k k k k k k k k k

k k k

k k k

Trace and write each sound word. Tell what sound goes with each picture.

tick   honk   click

Ask a friend to circle your best k and underline a k that could be better.

Ask a Friend

58

Lesson 51 Name ____

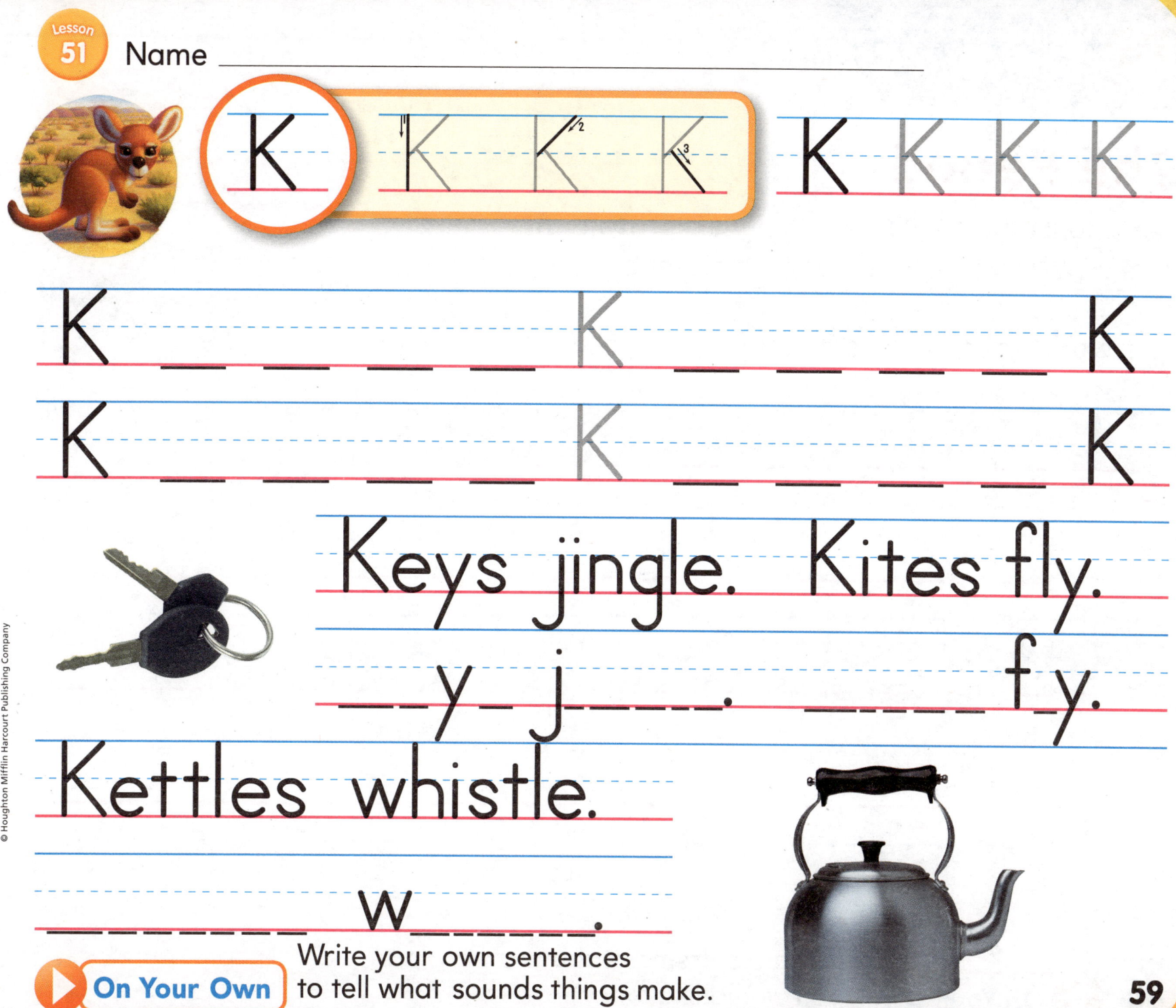

K K K K K K K K

K   K   K

K   K   K

Keys jingle.   Kites fly.
___y_ j_____.   ___ ___f_y.

Kettles whistle.
_____ w_____.

On Your Own — Write your own sentences to tell what sounds things make.

59

Lesson 52 Using Punctuation

Name _____

The Period

A sentence that tells something is a **statement.** Use a period at the end of a statement.

Trace and write each sentence.

The meal looked good.

Harry smelled the onions.

On Your Own Write a statement about a new food you would like to try.

Lesson 53 **Using Punctuation**

Name _____

The Question Mark

A sentence that asks something is a **question.**
A question ends with a question mark.
Trace and write the rows of question marks.
Then write the question.

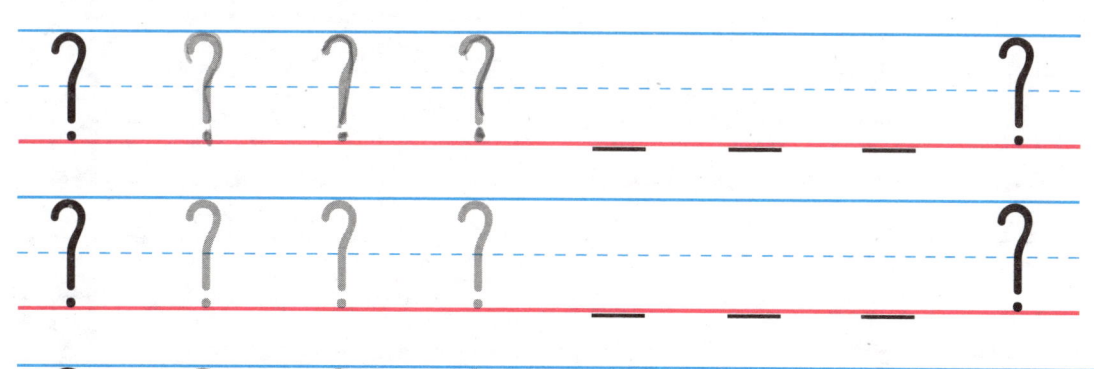

? ? ? ? _ _ _ ?

? ? ? ? _ _ _ ?

? ? ? ? _ _ _ _ ?

Do you like to cook?

_ _ y u _ _ _ _ c _ _ _

▶ **On Your Own** Write a question about a food.

61

Lesson 54

Name _____

b b b b b b

b   b   b
b   b   b
b   b   b

top   above   bottom   below
__ p   __ v   _____   __ w

62 **On Your Own** Make a list of other word pairs that are opposites.

Lesson 55 Name _____

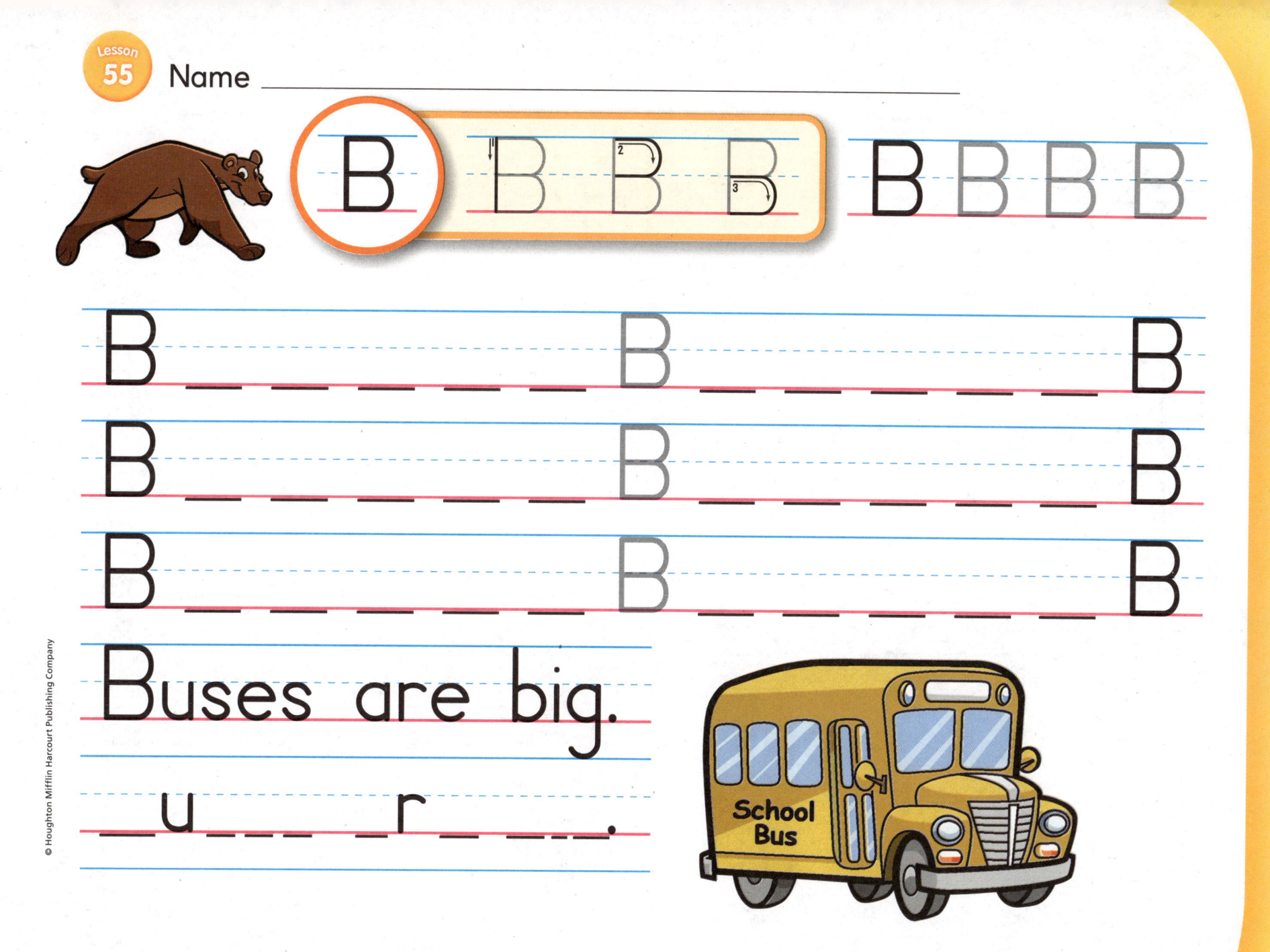

B B B B B B B B

B   B   B
B   B   B
B   B   B

Buses are big.
___u___ ___r_____.

Self Check Circle a B that has top and bottom loops the same size.

63

Lesson 56   Name _____

p p p p p p p p p

p   p   p

p   p   p

p   p   p

push   pull   stop   go
_u_   _u_

64 Ask a Friend — Ask a friend to circle your best p.

Lesson 57 Name _____

P P P P P P P P P

P P P

P P P

P P P

Pablo is happy.   Pat is sad.

_____y._____   _____._____

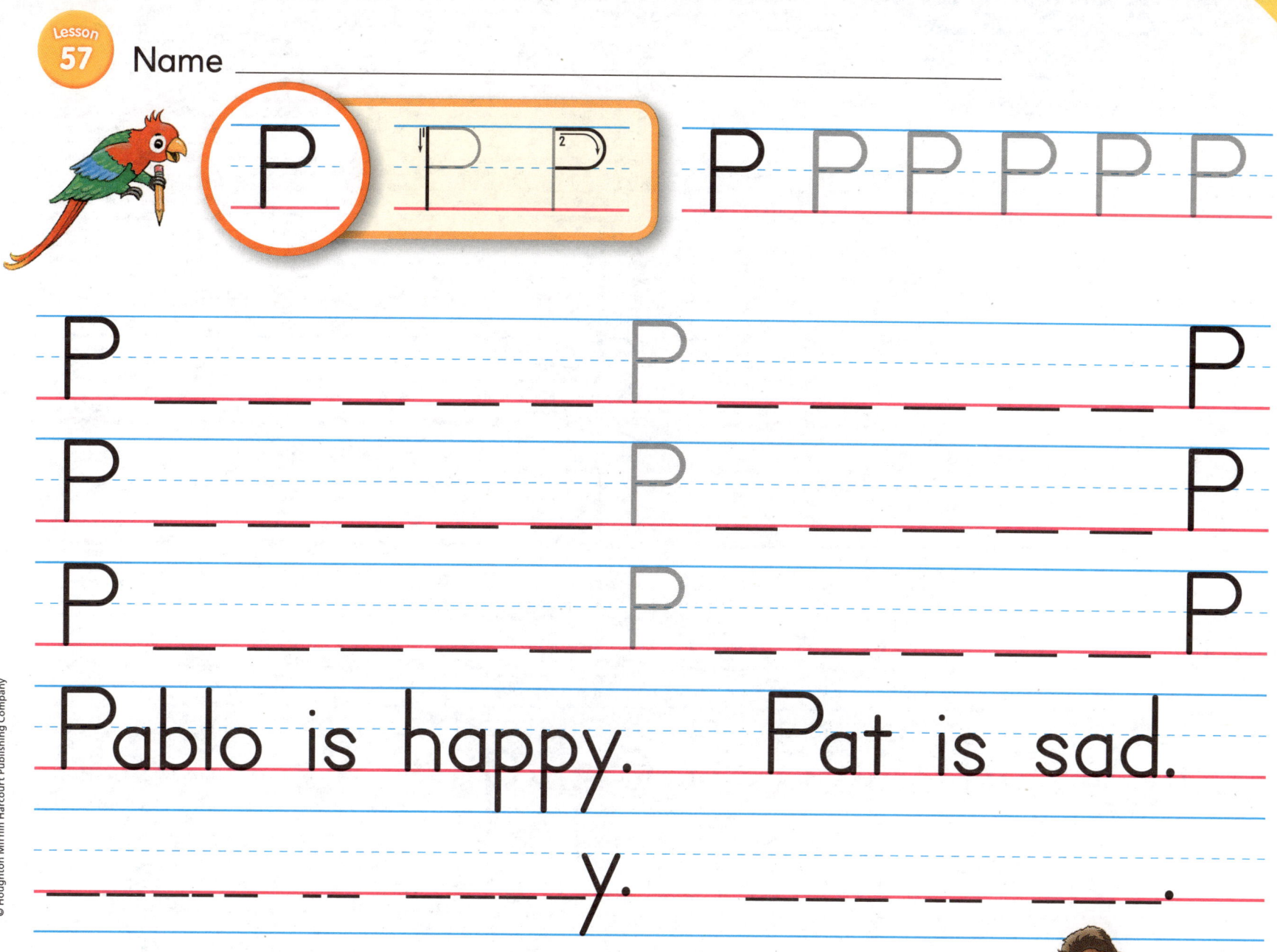

On Your Own — Write some sentence pairs that use opposites to describe two houses.

Lesson 58 Practice Name _____

P _ _ _ _ _ _ _ _	P _ _ _ _ _ _ _ _

b _ _ _ _ _ _ _ _	B _ _ _ _ _ _ _ _

k _ _ _ _ _ _ _ _	K _ _ _ _ _ _ _ _

h _ _ _ _ _ _ _ _	H _ _ _ _ _ _ _ _

Billy pitched the ball.
___ y ___ t e ___ t ___ a l.

Teacher's Directions: Have students write the missing letters.

Evaluation Name _____

Write each sentence.

Pam plants beans.

Bill picks them.

Circle the capital letter you wrote best.

Circle the word you wrote best.

Lesson 59

Name _____

r r r r r r r r r r r

r   r   r

r   r   r

r   r   r

red   rojo   green   verde

j_____   v_____

68   **Self Check**   Circle your best r.

Lesson 60 Name _____

R R R R R R R

R R R
R R R
R R R

Rosa has a red parrot.

On Your Own — Write another sentence that tells more about Rosa's parrot.

Lesson 61

Name _____

f f f f f f f f

f   f   f

f   f   f

f   f   f

furry brown bears

_u_ _y_ __w__ ____

Ask a Friend Have a friend circle one of your f's that is crossed at the midline.

70

Lesson 62 Name ___

F F F F F F F F

F F F

F F F

Four furry brown bears looked for berries.

__u__ __u__ __y__ __w__ _____

_____.

On Your Own Write another sentence that tells what one of the bears did.

71

Lesson 63

Name _____

u u u u u u u u u

u u u

u u u

u u u

smooth fur   soft purr

72 ▶ On Your Own   Write a riddle for an animal on this page.

Lesson 64

Name _____

u u u u u u u u u

u u u

u u u

Under the house
I found a mouse.

Self Check Circle your best u.

73

Lesson 65

Name _____

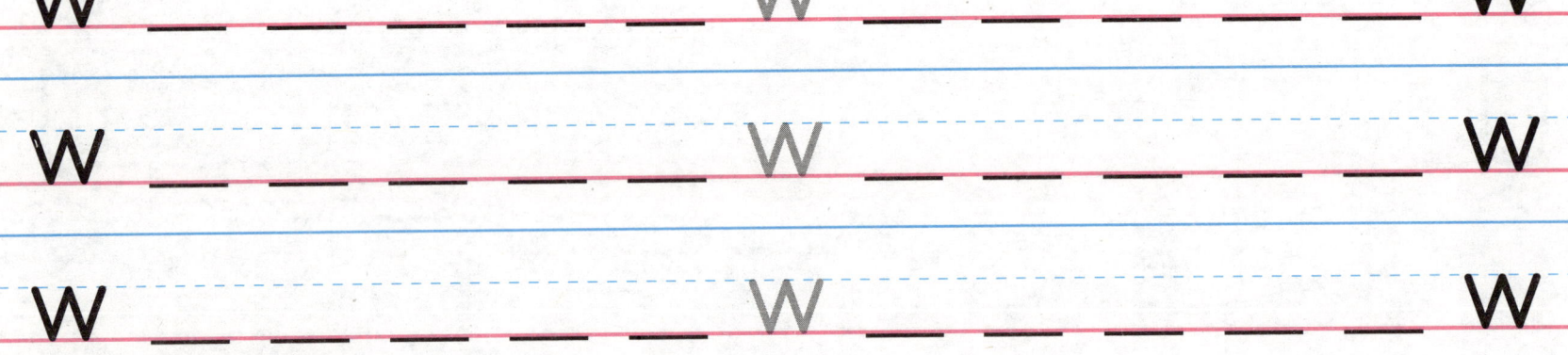

w w w w w w w w

w   w   w

w   w   w

w   w   w

The paw has claws.

On Your Own Make a list of words that describe different kinds of cats.

74

Lesson 66

Name _____

W

W   W   W

W   W   W

W   W   W

Where will I nap?
Warm, under a hat.

Ask a Friend Ask a friend to circle your best W.

75

Lesson 67 Practice   Name _____

r _____ R _____ u _____ U _____

f _____ F _____ w _____ W _____

The dog's fur was wet.

_ e __ o ____ a _ t.

Teacher's Directions: Have students write the missing letters.

Evaluation Name _____

Write the paragraph.

Wags is our dog. He is brown. Wags runs fast. He is the fastest dog around.

Lesson 68 Name _____

y y y y y y y y

y — — — y — — — y

y — — — y — — — y

Many years ago there was a little mouse.

Rewrite the sentence.
Change *mouse* to another animal.

Lesson 69

Name _____

Y

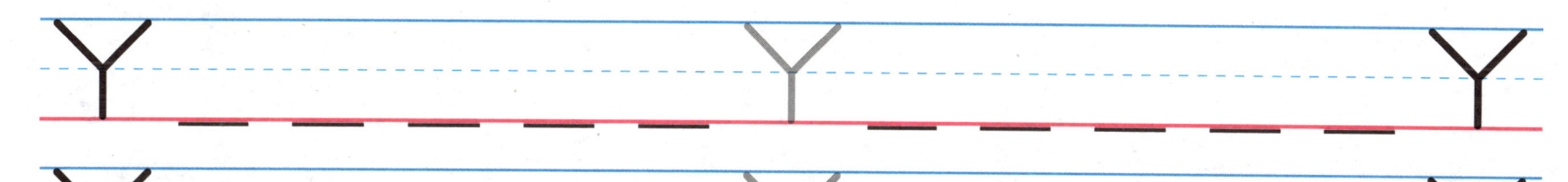

His name was was Yuri.
Yuri was kind.

On Your Own — Write the sentence again. Change the underlined word to another word that describes a person or an animal.

79

Lesson 70 Name ___

v v v v v v v v v v

v v v

v v v

v v v

Nearby lived five cats.

On Your Own — Write the sentence again. Change the underlined word to something else that might live nearby.

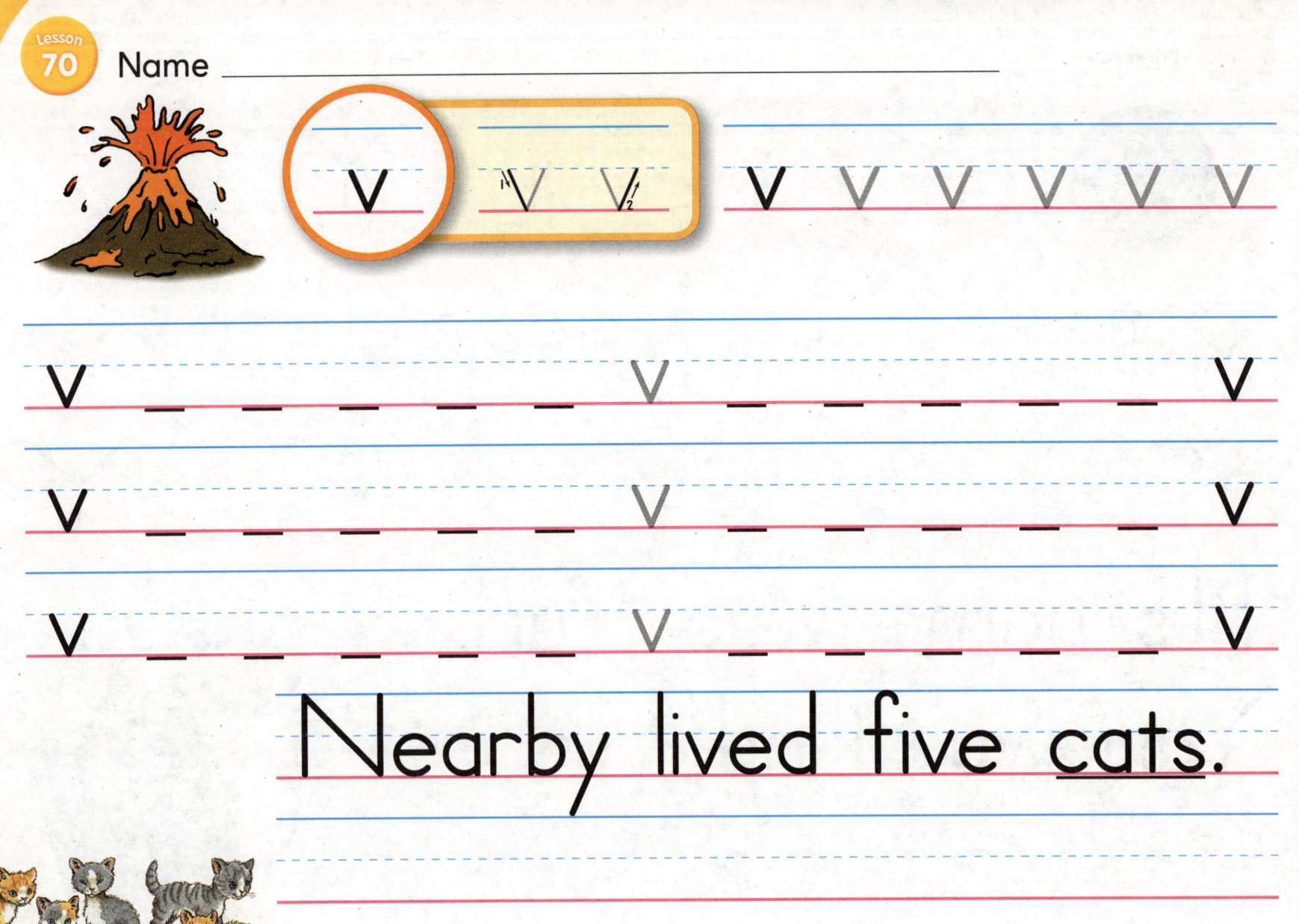

80

Lesson 71 Name _____

V

Very soon there was trouble.

Self Check Circle the word with the best spacing between letters.

81

Lesson 72

Name _____

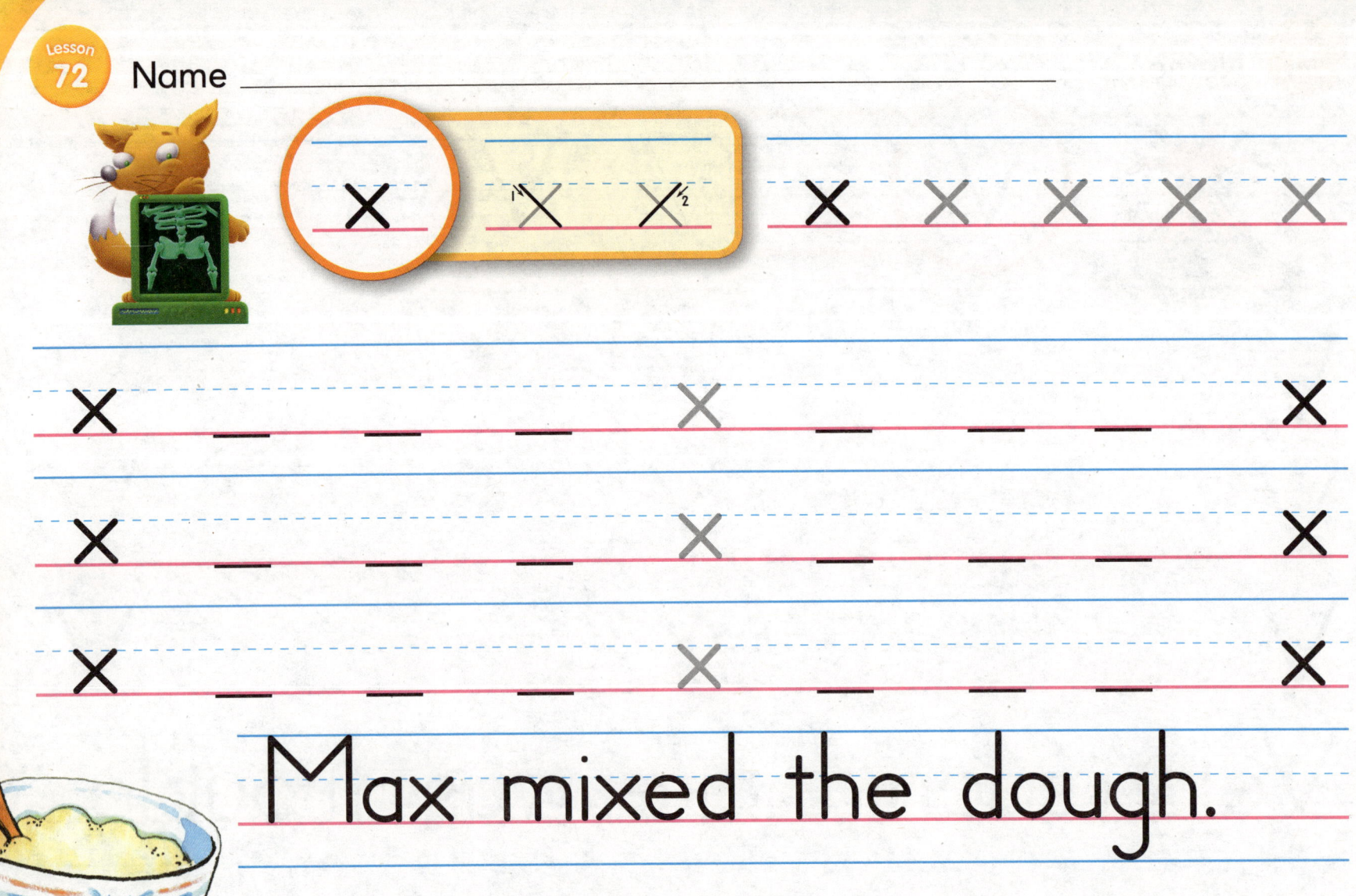

X x x X X X X X

X   x   X

X   x   X

X   x   X

Max mixed the dough.

On Your Own Tell about a time you worked with someone to prepare a special meal.

Lesson 73

Name _____

X X X X X X X

X   X   X
X   X   X
X   X   X

Xavier fixed the toppings.

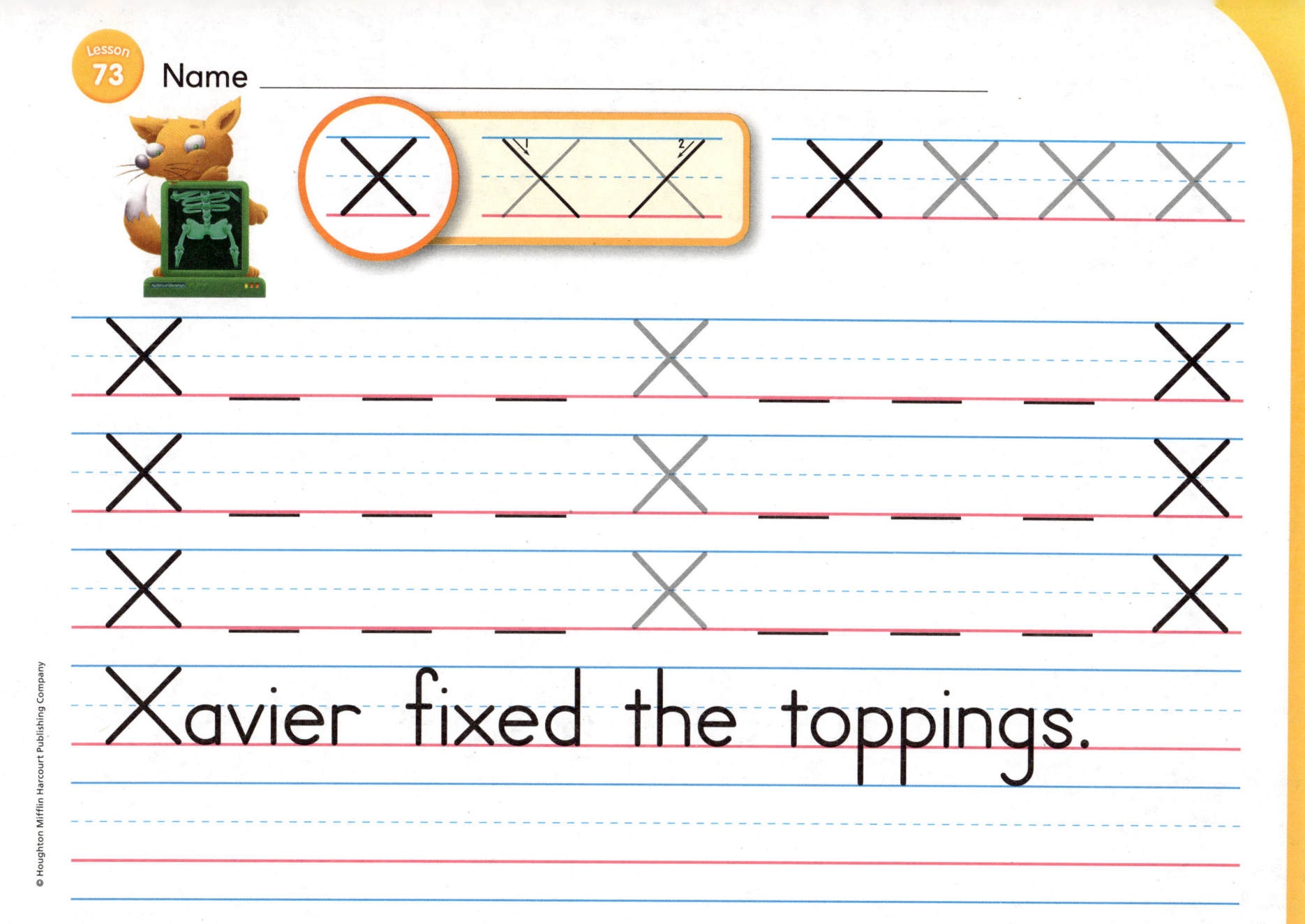

Self Check Circle the word with the best spacing between letters.

83

Lesson 74

Name _____

z z z z z z z z z z

z   z   z

z   z   z

z   z   z

Liza made pizza sauce.

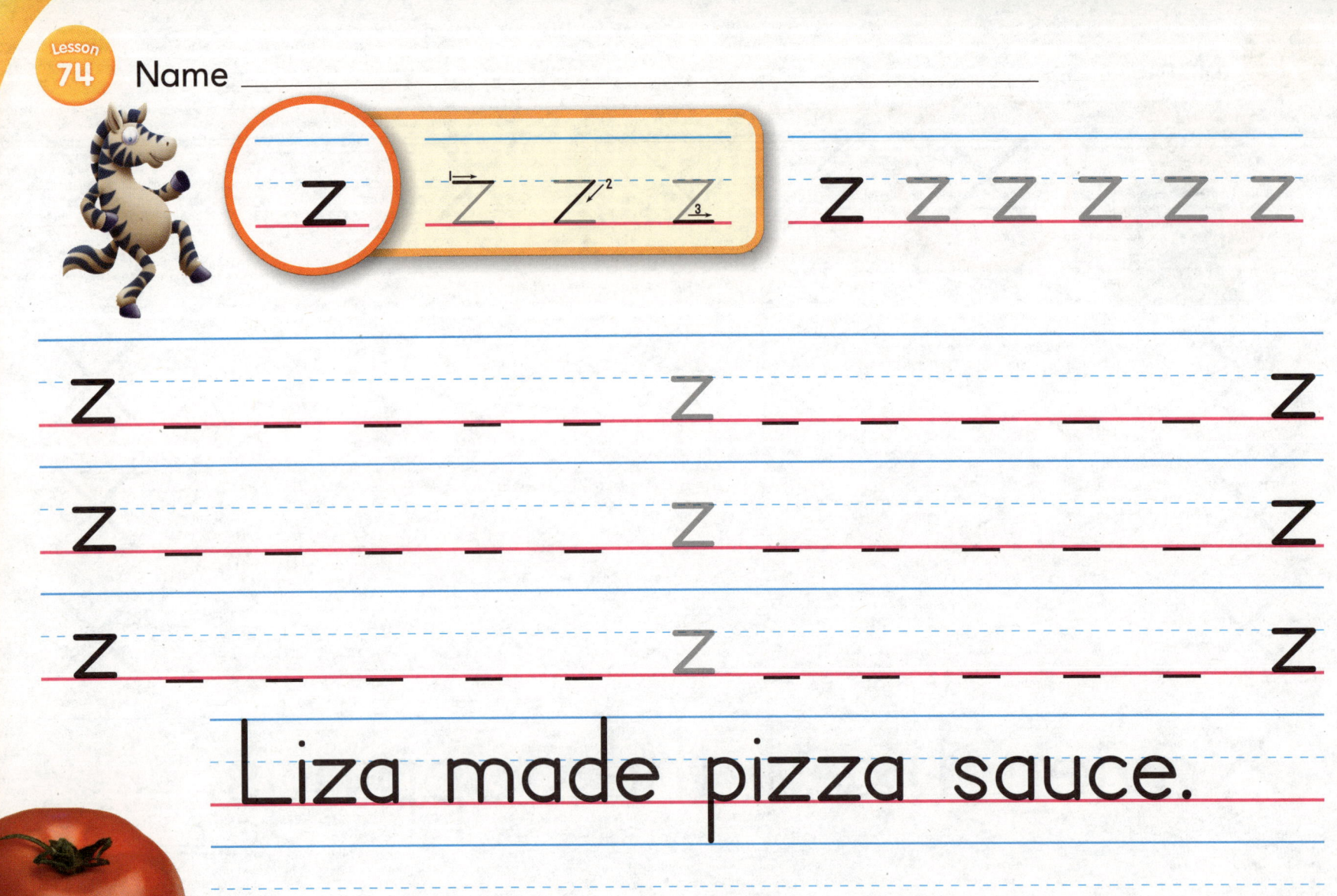

84 Ask a Friend — Have a friend circle the word with the best spacing between letters.

Lesson 75

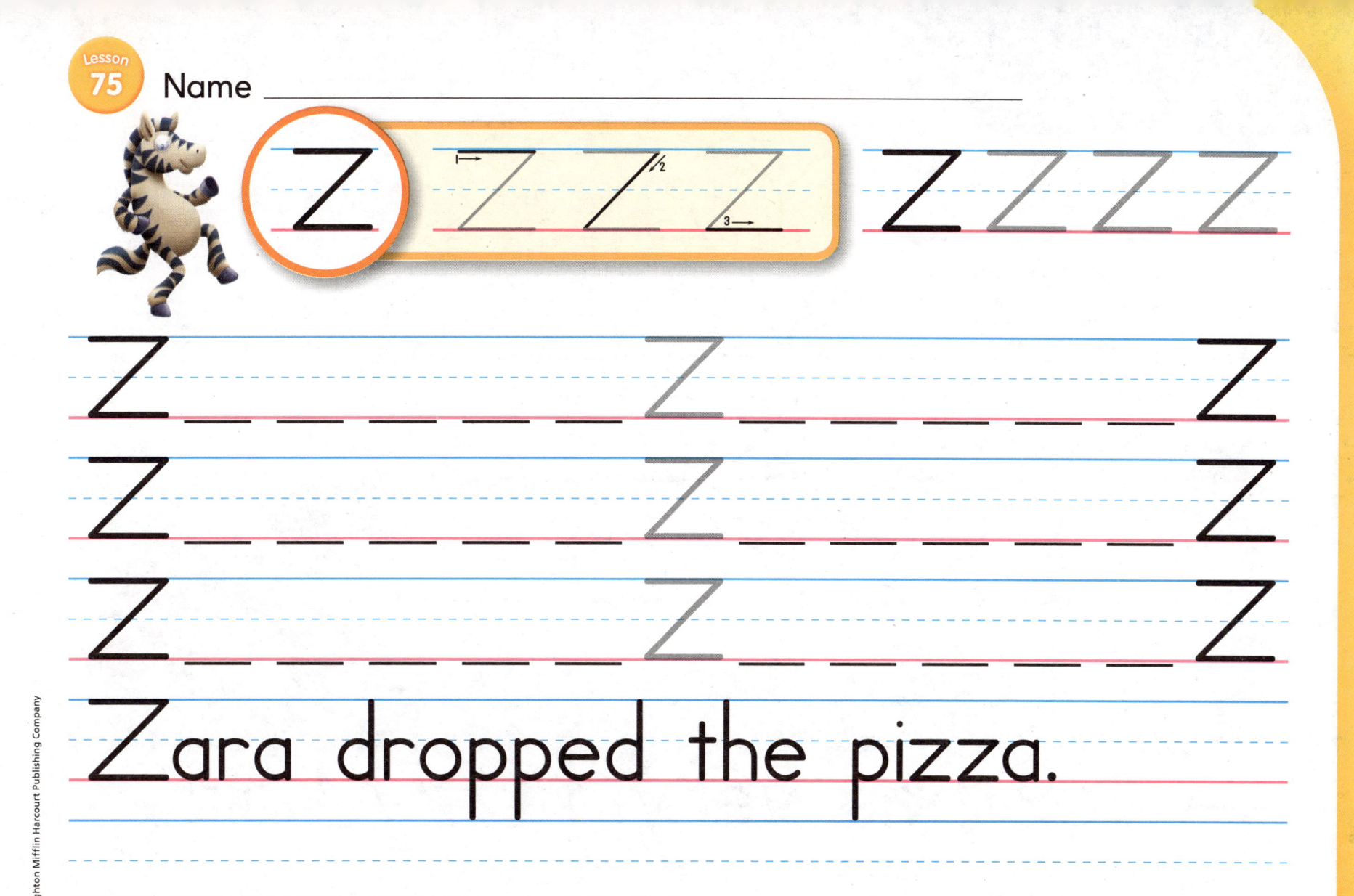

Name _____

Z z z Z z z z z

Z z Z

Z z Z

Z z Z

Zara dropped the pizza.

On Your Own — Make a list of toppings you would put on a pizza.

85

Lesson 76 Practice

Name _____

y _____   Y _____
v _____   V _____
x _____   X _____
z _____   Z _____

A fox has very fuzzy hair.
A_o_ _a_ _e_ _u_ _ai_.

Teacher's Directions: Have students write the missing letters.

Evaluation Name _____

Write these sentences.

Alex fixed a tasty stew.
Zelda took it to the zoo.
Zack liked it. Did you?

Circle the word you wrote best.

Circle a word that has all the letters spaced correctly.

Lesson 77

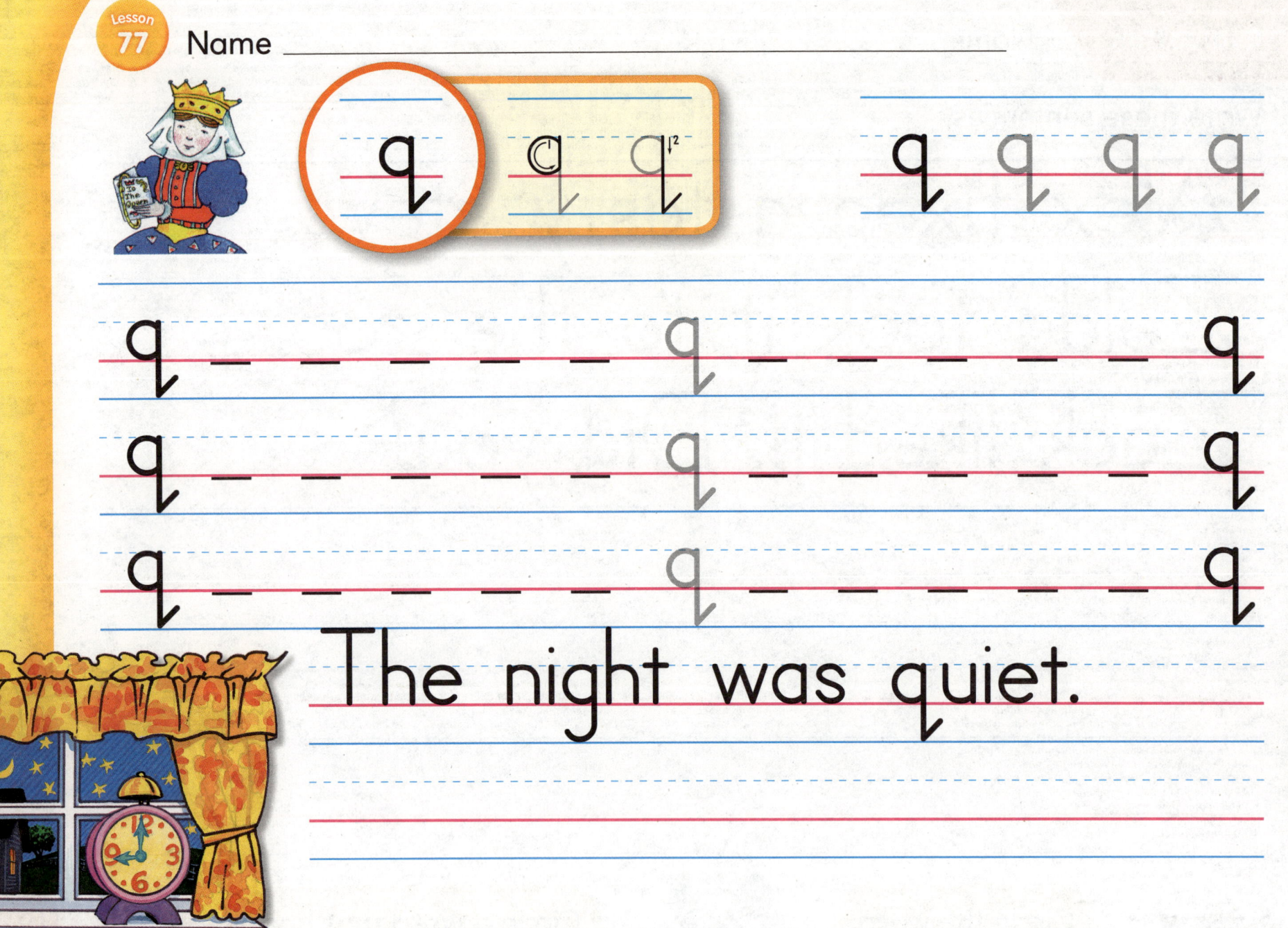

Name _____

q   q   q   q q q q

q   q   q

q   q   q

q   q   q

The night was quiet.

Invite a friend to circle any q's that do not touch the descender line.

88 ▶ Ask a Friend

Lesson 78

Name _____

Q Q Q Q Q Q Q

Q Q Q
Q Q Q
Q Q Q

Quinn likes square dances.

On Your Own — What do you think might happen at the square dance? Write your ideas.

89

Lesson 79 Name _____

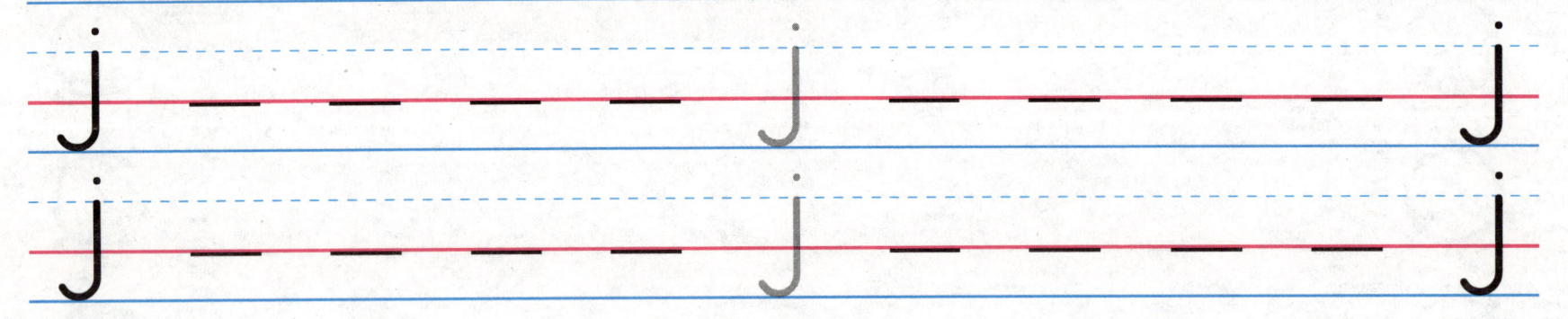

j j j j j j j

j — — — j — — — j

j — — — j — — — j

The jamboree just started.

90 **Self Check** — Circle a place where the spacing between words could be better.

Lesson 80 Name _____

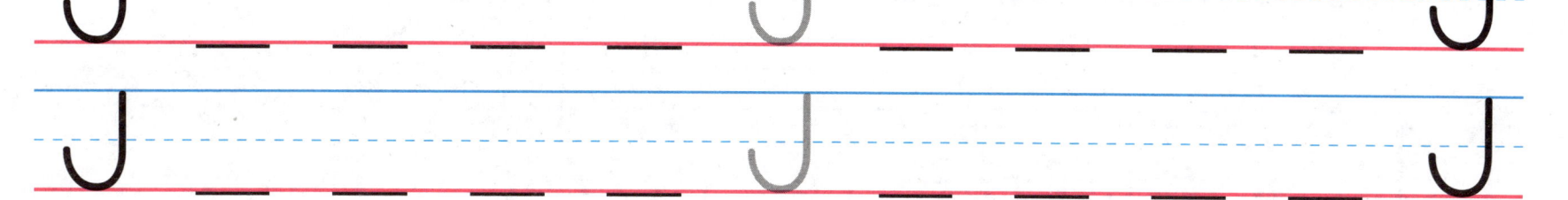

J J J J J J J

J J J

J J J

Jenny played her banjo.
Juan smiled and danced.

On Your Own Write how you think the story might end.

91

Handwriting Problems

Some handwriting is hard to read. Here are some reasons why.

Curved strokes are too straight.

Letters are not closed

Miles made an cuyle.

Loops are added.

Tell what makes this handwriting hard to read.

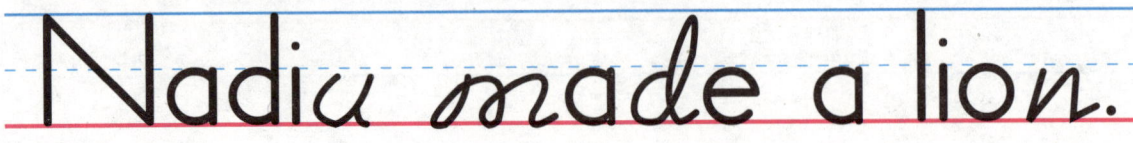

Nadiu made a lion.

92

Handwriting Feature

Name _____

Personal Style

There is no one in the world quite like you. You walk, talk, think, act, and dress in your own special way.

You write in your own special way, too. Look at the size of the words below.

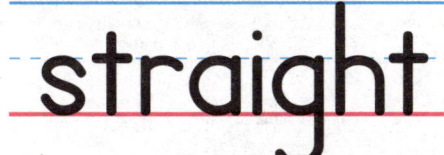

wide

narrow

straight

Use your personal style to write your name.

Evaluation Name _____

Write these sentences.

Quincy jumped for joy.

Jan liked the quilt.

Jack ran quickly.

Circle the word you wrote best.

Circle a word that has all the letters spaced correctly.

94